FLAGSTAFF'S WALKUP FAMILY MURDERS

A Shocking 1937 Tragedy

SUSAN JOHNSON

THE History PRESS

Published by The History Press
Charleston, SC
www.historypress.com

Front cover: Scene within the highland and high-desert terrain of northern Arizona; above the city of Flagstaff. *Library of Congress (loc.gov).*

First published 2021

Manufactured in the United States

ISBN 9781467147156

Library of Congress Control Number: 2021941622

For Paul, who told me I was a writer—and needed to write.

And for John, Rose, Daniel and Phoebe,
whose short lives were too easily forgotten.

CONTENTS

PREFACE

Over a decade ago, in a world unfamiliar with the word *Covid* and an easiness in life I now miss, my husband and I anted up the fee to walk through Flagstaff's historic Citizens Cemetery on a self-guided tour. The monies benefitted the Arizona Historical Society, one of their seasonal fund-raisers that we enjoyed doing together. It was a beautiful fall day that those of us who live here revel in—cool and breezy with a warm sun overhead. We walked between the different plots, many with third- or fourth-generation descendants on site, and enjoyed the anecdotes and tall tales they shared. At some point we meandered into the old Masonic section and stopped at a slightly raised grave with a single gentleman in attendance. He introduced himself as Joseph Jordan and revealed he wasn't a family member but rather a member of the historical society. There were, he said ominously, no relatives who survived those buried beneath the two markers in the double plot.

That was my introduction to the sad, tragic story of the Walkup family who lived in Flagstaff during the 1920s and '30s. As Jordan told the story—albeit in an abbreviated fashion—I found myself fascinated and filled with questions. I asked him the obvious ones, but eventually he looked at me and, with a twinkle in his eye, said: "You should go to the library and look the story up." No doubt a teacher at heart!

I began to do exactly what he suggested, at first pouring through the microfilm on a rare weekend off and later delving deeper into the story as background for a seasonal ghost tour. The more information I found, the more questions I had and even researching this book hasn't answered all of them. One of the most disturbing discoveries I've made is that this once prominent family has been forgotten—very few people have heard their story. Locals who have been here for generations were perplexed when I asked about the Walkup family.

"You mean the dome?" they'd ask. Most thought I was referring to Northern Arizona University's Walkup Skydome, an indoor sports stadium named after J. Lawrence Walkup, who is no relation to the Walkups in this story. This alone causes a bit of consternation; how can two families named Walkup not be related?

In retrospect, the town can be forgiven for not knowing the Walkups of 1937. There's been very little mention of the family after that warm July evening, and as one longtime resident said, "Why air our dirty laundry?" To that end, this book aims to shed a ray of light on the tragic events and remember the lives that were lost. Hopefully I've done that without a lot of sensationalism. The book also tries to paint a picture of life in this semi-isolated mountain town during the early twentieth century. While it's hard to say just how much influence time, geography and community had on the events, I believe each contributed at least something to the outcome.

To paraphrase Carl Jung, that which is in the shadows often drives us, even if unconsciously. While I personally don't believe the events of 1937 are reverberating through the community today, I can't help wondering how a book about the Walkup tragedy would have been received if written in the 1960s. Flagstaff's population hadn't yet exploded and many of the residents would have once been the Walkup children's schoolmates. Did they, like the town of the '40s, bury the memory of their friends? Or did they occasionally talk among themselves about John, Rose, Danny and Elizabeth? Where did they file away the horror of that summer's evening in their minds, so as to keep moving forward? Like so many questions regarding this sad drama, there are few concrete answers.

I hope this book tweaks the reader's curiosity and expands your knowledge about life a century ago in this small mountain town. It was a unique period in Arizona's history, and especially Flagstaff's. The citizens here strongly identified with the rugged individualism of the Wild West, but they were also influenced by the culture of surrounding communities and the many educational facilities established in town. Regardless of what conclusions you reach about the Walkups, they lived through historic times and the parents met the challenges as best they could. It is gratifying to know that they, and especially the Walkup children, have been remembered and their story told.

ACKNOWLEDGEMENTS

It has taken a village to write this book. Whether due to the pandemic or my inexperience as a writer, it's been difficult to research using online sources. I discovered that many resources have not been digitalized, but whenever I called on our local librarians, they responded quickly. They were pleasant and helpful and did their best to sift through the microfilm for an odd bit of information. They also photographed several of the images found in the book from issues of the *Coconino Sun*. Many thanks to Pam, Suzannah and Alexis—they're why we all love the library! And while I never made it back to NAU's Special Collections after January, the staff there was just as helpful. They allowed the use of an aerial view of the original Flagstaff Country Club in the book, and I am so appreciative of that.

Before I get into personal acknowledgments, I need to credit the Flagstaff newspaper that predated today's *Daily Sun*, the *Coconino Sun*. While I spent hours in the library going through microfilm, issues of the *Sun*—up to 1927—can be found online at the Library of Congress site as well as newspapers.com. This weekly paper informed my knowledge of life in early 1900s Flagstaff and provided many of the details of JD Walkup's involvement with the town. I came to think of the newspaper as another character in this book. The *Daily Sun* was generous in allowing the use of images for this book of past *Coconino Sun* issues—many thanks.

My friend John Propster was a fount of knowledge regarding photographs, and he patiently helped me slog through questions about formatting them. He also loaned a camera—thank you, John. Flagstaff artist—and writer—Karen Raskin-Young also helped with images, and I love the paintings she did of the Walkups.

Flagstaff's Right-Time Writers have been steadfast in their support as I've struggled through the process and were a stabilizing presence throughout the pandemic. Our weekly Zooms have been therapeutic for us all and personally kept me on track with this book. I am so proud and happy to be a member of this writing group—thank you all!

I want to thank Dr. Karen Renner, who encouraged me to write the book proposal for the Walkup murders; I wouldn't have thought to even try without her suggestion. I'm also grateful to Dr. Elizabeth Caspian, who shared her insights and expertise on questions I had regarding psychological aspects of this tragedy. I thoroughly enjoyed discussing the Walkups with her and—even though my editor warned against indulging in it too much—speculating on the events.

Speaking of editors, many thanks to mine, Laurie Krill, for being willing to take a chance on me. Not only was she encouraging, but she was also understanding and patient with several delays attributed to COVID-19. Thank you, Laurie.

Keith Robinson is one of the few people in Flagstaff who was as taken with the Walkups as I was. Keith wrote a paper on the family, which he shared with me before donating his works to NAU's Special Collections. I relied on a surprising amount of his research as offices, libraries and other resource centers closed down during the pandemic. I also quoted from his paper, which I enjoyed reading numerous times. I tried in vain to convince him to co-author this book; turns out he's a busy man. Thank you for your generosity, Keith.

Many thanks to Jack Welch for showing me the old golf course and sharing stories he collected from his fellow hikers and walkers. And to those in town who answered my emails and snail mail from out of the blue—if I listed everyone, I'd forget someone—thank you all! There are so many people who expressed an interest in and encouragement for this book, and I sincerely hope you know that I appreciate you.

I'd be remiss not to mention my former supervisor turned dear friend and writing buddy, OJ. Thank you for believing in me, encouraging me, asking about my progress—I wish you were here to read the result.

There are also people who, without their help, this book could not have been written. So, to my good friend Gwen—thank you for your steady encouragement, for your generosity in sharing sources, your kindness and interest in the Walkups and for being a woman who enjoys a good historical puzzle. And my unending gratitude goes out to Carleen, who, besides being a true friend, is a lifelong writer and published author. She listened to me read through paragraphs and offered gentle critiques to my writing that improved the story tremendously. Thank you, Carleen—I wish you lived closer.

And finally, I'm grateful to my sweet son who—thrown in with his mother during a pandemic while she was writing her first book—stayed remarkably cool and calm. I'm sure your dad is proud of us both.

INTRODUCTION

The Spring of 1937

Flagstaff, Arizona—a sleepy little railroad encampment that grew into a full-fledged town—enjoyed a wet, snowy winter that year. Residents were shaking off the cold and looking forward to the festivals and parades that came each summer. Baseball and softball featured prominently in the local press, with various teams occupying front-page status in the *Coconino Sun*, Flagstaff's weekly newspaper. The city fathers had resumed their search for a reliable water source to quench the ever-expanding community with its booming tourist industry. The population of five thousand seemed to be optimistic that spring as they went about their lives at the base of the San Francisco Peaks. After all, the Depression was over, and Flagstaff had weathered it better than most towns its size.

The city's post-Depression recovery was due partially to its diversified economy and careful management of resources. Records show that by 1935, any man who was able to work had a job. Tourism was on the rise, and Route 66 meandered through the city's south side, which sprouted motels and cafés seemingly overnight. Hollywood had reappeared, using the Hotel Monte Vista (or the Monte V as it's affectionately known) as a staging area for the popular Westerns filmed just outside of Flagstaff. On the west side of town atop Mars Hill, Lowell Observatory attracted world-class astronomers eager for a look through Percival Lowell's telescopes. Joseph Dolan had taken

Above: Humphrey's Peak, located in the Kachina Peaks Wilderness, is synonymous in the minds of many residents with the city of Flagstaff. *Author's collection.*

Opposite: This tintype photo of Lowell Observatory's entrance depicts the symbols of the nine planets. *Courtesy Freaky Foot Tours, photographer Eric Retterbush.*

over the sawmills and had both sides running, so local men were once again employed processing lumber.[1]

James Douglas Walkup, known better as JD, had a hand in planning many of the summer festivals that year, most notably the Fourth of July Powwow. As chairman of the County Board of Supervisors and a member of the Flagstaff Chamber of Commerce, JD was deeply involved in the hustle and bustle of the growing town. The *Sun* kept close tabs on all of the city's leaders, including Walkup, and reported on the frequent luncheons and meetings that filled his days as he went about his civic duties. Most of JD's activities were related to the business of overseeing county budgets and programs and promoting tourism. There were, however, always ceremonials and conventions in the works that appreciated the handsome gentleman's presence. It was a rare week that went by without some mention of JD Walkup on page one of the *Sun*.[2]

It's a mystery what occupied the life of JD's pretty wife of twelve years, Thelma Marie Green Walkup, in the spring of 1937. To be fair, a thirty-two-year-old mother of four children, aged ten and under, probably had her hands full most days. According to newspaper accounts the family had help from Alice Weston, known as La La, but it's not known if she assisted Marie with the household, the children or both. What is clear in the months leading up to July 22 is that Marie was not attending any of the countless dinner parties and celebrations reported in the social columns of the *Sun*. She was not a member of the women's golf league that played at the country club, nor did she sit in with any of the afternoon bridge clubs, of which there were several. Marie Walkup's name was not among those ladies attending teas, showers, sewing circles and flower shows. Nor is there any mention of her in connection with church-sponsored benefits or service organizations. For the wife of a prominent man about town—who *was* active in the various clubs—Marie seems to have been invisible that year, as well as most of the preceding ones.

Neither JD nor Marie were natives of Flagstaff. James hailed from Nashville, Tennessee, and came west after World War I; Marie was a transplant from Nebraska. They met and married in 1925, and by 1937,

Railroad Avenue in 1943, across from the train depot. The buildings are still identifiable today. *Library of Congress online catalog, photographer Jack Delano.*

they were a family of six residing in a two-story house on posh North Leroux Street. Their 1,500-square-foot home was situated on a large corner lot that also hosted a detached garage and small guest house. All of the buildings still stand today, looking a little worse for wear but structurally the same. A deep-set front porch runs half the length of the house, a reminder that neighbors once gathered here to exchange gossip or rock gently outside in the evening air. The neighborhood itself was referred to as the "Nob Hill" of Flagstaff, a sly dig at the town's elite who resided on the steeply sloping Leroux.[3]

JD would have had a five-minute walk each morning to the heart of downtown, where most of his county business took place. The two older children, Daniel, age ten, and Rose, just shy of eight, would have walked to school during the year. The two youngest Walkups, four-year-old John and Elizabeth, eighteen months, would have been home with their mother. JD was frequently out of town in his capacity as chairman that year, usually in Phoenix. The Chamber of Commerce offices were also located downtown in the Hotel Monte Vista, and JD was so involved in his position there that it was almost a second job. While one can presume from her husband's schedule that Marie was often alone with the children, she was far from trapped. Flagstaff was quite walkable those years, and the Walkups owned at least one family car.

Many factors played into the day of reckoning that was to come that summer. There was the softball fever that lit up the town, JD's increasing absences as he carefully maneuvered his career and Marie's continued isolation from the social events of the day. Sometime in late June or early July, Marie developed a stomach ailment that Dr. Fronske attempted to treat, with little success. Whether she was truly ill or was falling prey to some inner anxiety (as Fronske later intimated), the end result was something no one in this small mountain town was prepared for.

1

A MOUNTAIN TOWN AND ITS PEOPLE

Before proceeding any further it's important to acknowledge that this is the Anglicized version of Flagstaff's beginnings. Native American tribes lived here for many centuries before the Europeans arrived. It would be impossible to detail their rich history and heritage in any one book, and certainly not by this author. Suffice it to say there are volumes already written that tell the story of the Sinagua, Hopi, Navajo and other tribes by historians of the area.

Northern Arizona's mild yet snowy winters and cool, sunny summers had caught the eye of sheep herders and ranchers in the mid-nineteenth century. Many of these families had been moving west along the Beale Wagon Road, driving their livestock and traveling on horseback or in wagons. They risked the dangers of the unknown because they were headed to the promised land of lush green grasses and temperate climate—California. As they passed through this high desert land at the base of the snow-covered San Francisco Peaks, it made an impression in some of their minds. When a prolonged drought, followed by swarms of locusts, hit California in 1875, a sheep herder by the name of Thomas McMillian decided to turn his remaining flock around and retrace his steps along Beale's Road. He arrived in what is now Flagstaff in 1876 and claimed the grasslands around the Peaks as his homestead. McMillian was soon joined by others—Frank Hart, John Elden and Charles O'Neill to name but a few. These ranchers saw the potential of this high desert valley where livestock could graze all summer and then be driven south sixty or so miles to the low desert for winter. However, even though the ranchers were credited with being the first white settlers, it was the railroad and surrounding forest that marked the town's potential and cemented its place in history.[4]

In 1880, the front men from the Atlantic-Pacific Railroad arrived at what became known as Old Town in Flagstaff. They were surveying land and prepping the railbed for track as the railroad continued its westward march. They were soon followed by hundreds of workers and, as the noise and activity increased, so did the saloons and gambling halls. Most of the men moved on with the work, a few stayed in town and after the rail system was completed in California, a number of them returned. The biggest draw besides the clean mountain air and stunning landscape was the opportunity for work at the Ayer Lumber Company.

E.E. Ayer was a businessman from Chicago who had worked for the railroad in the past. On a scouting expedition he saw the vast ponderosa pine forest surrounding the tiny settlement and immediately recognized its potential. He returned to the area with all the parts and machinery to construct a steam-powered sawmill and was open for business less than three weeks after the first train chugged its way through town.

The historic downtown train depot was built in 1926 and is still in service today. The station also houses the Flagstaff Visitor Center. *Courtesy Freaky Foot Tours, tintype photography by Eric Retterbush.*

The sawmill secured Flagstaff's future, offering good wages and steady employment for decades. The men who were married sent for their wives and children; those who were single had a future to offer a prospective mate. A town that has families is a community that needs churches, schools, shops and stores. The first schoolhouse—a one-room, multi-class clapboard—was opened in 1883. The churches soon followed and while they were heavily outnumbered by the saloons and gambling halls, the temperate hand of the town's educated leaders was becoming evident in the landscape.

Ayers was soon ready to hand off the mill to a solid manager so that he could pursue other interests. Denis Riordan was a capable young Navajo Indian agent who was interested in quitting his government job and learning the lumber business. Riordan was a quick study and soon brought his two half-brothers out west to join him. Timothy and Michael Riordan eventually bought out their brother's share of the mill and made their home in Flagstaff. They became important members of the community, holding public office and keeping the mill running. In 1903, the brothers, who had married the two sisters Caroline and Elizabeth Metz, hired Charles Whittlesey to design and build an American Arts and Crafts–style house. It was actually two separate homes connected by a large common area that was used as a ballroom or game room by the families. This beautiful historic house still stands today in an area designated Riordan Mansion State Historic Park, which sits perilously close to a Northern Arizona University parking garage.[5]

If the Riordans were synonymous with lumber in Flagstaff, the Babbitt brothers were and are still known for their civic involvement and mercantile successes in town. Two of the five brothers, David and William, arrived here in 1886 from Ohio. They were successful businessmen in Cincinnati, and the brothers wanted to expand their holdings out west. After surveying the land, they bought a herd of cattle and sent for the remaining brothers, C.J., George and Edward. While they made a fortune with their livestock, they also operated automobile dealerships, department stores and Indian trading posts. Interestingly, the Babbitts and the Riordans were related through marriage, as Caroline and Elizabeth Metz were cousins of the Babbitt brothers.[6]

The early influence of these two families, as well as several others that are still in town, is difficult to over-stress. Both families were composed of well-educated, sober, civic-minded people who valued stability and family life. As the prominent citizens of their day, they laid a solid foundation for the town to follow. By all accounts, members of both families had their quirks and

A street view of Michael Riordan's home, which adjoins his brother Tim's to create the thirteen-thousand-square-foot Riordan Mansion State Historic Park. The turn-of-the-century home was built in the Arts and Crafts style and included running water and electricity. *Author's collection.*

character flaws; they were also known to enjoy a good prank and a shot or two of whiskey on occasion. However, the Riordans and Babbitts invested in the town's schools, churches and infrastructure. Many a railroad town boomed and went bust because of the lack of discipline and leadership. Flagstaff not only survived but immediately began to thrive as the sawmill turned out lumber for buildings and railroad ties. Steady growth and happy employees helped keep the town on the track forward. The Flagstaff of 1890 paved the way for the Flagstaff of 1930 and is still evident in its values today.

2

THELMA MARIE GREEN AND JD WALKUP

Very little background is available on Thelma Marie Green prior to her marriage to JD Walkup. She was born in North Platte, Nebraska, on June 2, 1905, to parents John H. and Story Cannon Green. She preferred the name Marie and had a brother John and a younger sister, Arietta. Whether the siblings were close is anyone's guess, but one of the letters at the crime scene was addressed to "Mama and Arietta." Newspaper accounts indicate the family moved to Flagstaff in 1916, when Marie was eleven years old. However, if the Greens did relocate that year there was no mention of that fact or of the family itself in the local paper. On June 2, 1916, one possible item was found in the Interesting Events in the Local Social World column written by Mrs. Frank N. Noble for the *Coconino Sun*. The blurb mentions a Mrs. Green who assisted in a luncheon at the Federated Church, the same building in which Marie would marry nine years later. Unlike most other entries regarding the town's women in Noble's columns, neither the husband's first name nor Mrs. Green's Christian name was used for further identification. Other than that, there is no mention about any Greens in Flagstaff that summer.[7]

For a small town of three thousand that was fairly isolated atop a mountain there was a lot happening the summer of 1916. Mrs. Noble's social column was filled with details on card parties, with bridge and five hundred being the favorite, and afternoon teas and luncheons. There were automobile parties that ended in picnics at Walnut Canyon or Sedona, as well as the requisite birthday celebrations and weddings. Flower arrangements

Established in 1916, the Flagstaff Federated Community Church endures today. This beautiful structure is made of Moenkopi sandstone—also known as Arizona Red. According to the newspaper, the Walkups were married in the parsonage. *Author's collection.*

were described in great detail, and one supposes Mrs. Noble had a penchant for gardening. Delicate white and pink sweet peas, golden posies, colorful carnations and even bursts of sunflowers were given high remarks in her weekly columns. Her preferred adjective for food, frocks and hand-painted cards was "dainty." The name of each partygoer and bridge club member was carefully recorded by Noble, who often added the titles "Mesdames" and "Messers" to indicate the proper social and marital status.[8]

Church activities were duly noted in the weekly paper, as the institution held an important role in weaving together the town's social fabric. The religious community was represented by all the established denominations: Roman Catholics, Episcopalians, Methodists and Mormons. There was a smaller contingency of Christian Scientists, Jews and Baptists, and no hostilities were recorded between members of the various faiths. The Federated Church seemed to be the institution in Flagstaff that drew in and connected people from all walks of life. Besides being a house of worship, it hosted secular meetings, local plays and various lectures to which the whole community was welcomed. The church still stands today, its Malapis rock foundation as sturdy as it was in 1916.

The main attractions that summer were the same as the year before and the decade that followed. Baseball was arguably the town's favorite pastime, with Flagstaff joining the national craze in 1895. The men formed a team

What Is It With Ball Games?

Flagstaff was just one more town consumed with baseball throughout the twentieth century. The sport earned its nickname "America's Pastime" honestly, as everyone from farm boys to soldiers played the game when an open field and a spare hour were found. Some enthusiasts claim the game's popularity was cemented during the Civil War as soldiers—far from home for the first time and thrown in with strangers—played baseball with makeshift equipment. The impromptu games were entertaining and built morale, and the young men brought the love of the game home.*

While Canada laid claim to the first recorded baseball game in 1838, the New York Knickerbockers played the first publicized game in the United States in October 1845. Some form of baseball can be traced back centuries earlier to Europe as the British and Germans enjoyed stick and ball games. The rules were different than those we know today, but the players and fans were just as enthusiastic. In the States, as clubs were divided into teams and the play required more skill, enthusiastic fans were willing to part with some coin to watch and cheer. The National League was formed in 1876 and the American League followed in 1882. It took a few decades of in-fighting and turmoil before something resembling the baseball of today appeared, but the sport only grew in popularity. When radio began calling the plays during the 1920s, people across the United States tuned in to cheer and boo from the comfort of their living rooms.†

While the history of baseball is well documented, the origins of softball are more obscure. According to a 1956 paper written by Irvin Kawarsky, the first mention of the game came out of Chicago in 1887. Members of a boat club were lazing about, waiting for updates from Western Union on a Yale-Harvard football game. As the score tightened, one of the men picked up an old boxing glove and threw it at an opposing fan. The other saw the glove coming and, having a wand in his hand, batted the glove away. This playful antic inspired the boys to mark off a diamond indoors, and, tying

* Miklich, "The Game," 19C Baseball.

† Ibid., "The Rules."

the glove into a ball with its own strings, they played a makeshift game of baseball. George Hancock was one of the young men at the Farragut Boat Club that day, and he and his friends went on to refine the game, called "indoor baseball," and play other teams in Chicago. It soon spread to other cities and states and became popular in its own right.*

As said before, Flagstaff was right there with the rest of the nation in its love for the game. Babbitt Brothers was just one of the local businesses to sponsor a team. Impromptu games were reported on in the *Sun* with about as much enthusiasm as awarded those in the National League. Loyal groups of fans showed up to watch throughout northern Arizona, cheering and booing and making an afternoon of it. Softball increased in popularity in the 1930s, with both men and women forming teams, and soon the game developed its own loyal crowd of supporters.

* Kawarsky, "Evolution and History." Kawarsky's paper on the evolution of softball was dated December 31, 1956, and was part of a requirement for his master's degree at Drake University in Iowa. Any fan of the game will enjoy both Dimitry's site and Kawarsky's interesting paper—both are full of obscure facts and entertaining trivia.

to compete against neighboring towns, and the game became a much anticipated and fiercely played sport every season. The *Sun* not only gave front-page space to the local play-by-play, but the cheering spectators were often hailed by name as they followed their team throughout Arizona. In the following decades, women's softball became almost as popular, and a regional playoff has a small role in the Walkup story.

Besides baseball, the Fourth of July celebrations were a highlight of the summertime. The summer holiday was replete with parades, dancing and a rodeo, which brought the Native American tribes into town to both watch and compete along with the residents. Navajo and Hopi ceremonial dances, which were open to the non-Native public, also occurred around midsummer and drew large crowds of onlookers. All of these activities were closely tied to Flagstaff's growing reputation as an eclectic yet cultured summer retreat from the heat and noise. The increased tourism was especially welcomed and already important to the town's economy. As the Greens settled into their new home that year, the community offered plenty of opportunity and activity. At age eleven, Marie would most likely have attended Emerson School that fall; however, there's no mention of her in any of the school programs.[9]

James Douglas Walkup, known locally as JD, was born on January 3, 1899, in Nashville, Tennessee. There's a caveat here: his birth year has been reported as both 1899 and 1900. I am going with the former, as it's engraved on his headstone at Fort Whipple National Cemetery in Prescott, Arizona. According to information from both a 1934 *Sun* endorsement and his 1972 obituary, JD received "a good education" in Nashville and later went to work at Keith Simman's Hardware Co. in Tennessee. When World War I broke out, he signed up and was shipped overseas with the Thirtieth Division. He fought in six major battles in Belgium and France. In the historic battle at Bellicourt, he was reportedly gassed and hit with machine gun fire. That was in September 1918, and soon afterward he returned stateside. Walkup joined a number of other veterans who came west in hopes that the cool, dry air would ease their breathing. In 1919 he moved to Prescott, Arizona, and landed a job as a buyer for a goat ranch. After several years, he migrated farther up the mountain to Flagstaff, where he took a job with Babbitt Brothers in one of their mercantile stores.[10]

The year before JD's arrival in town was marked by the end of World War I and a devastating flu pandemic. Flagstaff had proven itself patriotic during the Great War, rationing food and goods as directed, and hobbled through the influenza outbreak as best it could. Now it was bursting with ideas and optimism for getting back on its feet. Tourism was utmost in the town's mind when the business leaders considered Flagstaff's economy. In early 1923, the city was bombarding its citizens with the urgency of developing new water supplies and shoring up the existing structures. "Flagstaff's Future Growth Depends on Water Development" was a recurring headline in the paper. Providing enough water for the sawmills and railroads was equally as important as seeing to the needs of businesses and local homes. The town's people expected the council to grapple with the issue as they turned their attention to building and growth.

There's no immediate mention of Walkup's arrival in town in the *Sun*'s Local Brevities, the page that had now replaced Mrs. Nolan's column. That seems a little odd, as JD was described by one Platt Cline in his book *Mountain Town* as "a tall, good-looking fellow." One would think JD's appearance on the scene would create an immediate stir and be duly noted in the columns. To understand why, we need to look at the entity that was the *Coconino Sun* and the role it occupied in the town.[11]

3

THE WEEKLY NEWSPAPER

It would be difficult to over-stress the importance of the *Coconino Sun* in the life of 1900s Flagstaff. Published weekly from 1883 to 1946, the paper went to press Thursday evening and arrived on doorsteps and in stores Friday morning. A year's subscription could be had for two dollars in 1920 and three in 1930. Everything that was going on in northern Arizona was given space—from city and county business to new buildings downtown to reports on the collage and elementary schools. State and national news was also closely scrutinized and reported with an eye toward how the town was affected by any new legislation. Local crime was often on page one, and the names of jurors called for duty were printed there as well. To read a copy of the *Sun* was to know the issues facing Flagstaff in the early twentieth century and how the town was inclined to deal with them.

For a small mountain town that was snowbound several months a year, one could easily imagine social news was scant. As mentioned before, however, both the society page and Personals were filled each week with the kind of gossipy items that contradict that notion. Besides the teas and card parties, ailments of every kind and those afflicted were reported and commented on. During the flu pandemic of 1918 and for years afterward, the name of every townsperson who suffered from the virus was printed, as well as their condition. There was a practicality to that, of course; knowing if the town was in danger of a pandemic was vital. However, broken bones from falls, bloody noses, attacks of rheumatism—these incidents also filled the columns

THE COCONINO SUN

Society, Church and Club News

WOMAN'S CLUB MET AT HOME OF MRS. H. S. COLTON

State Federation In Convention At Williams Apr. 25-27

Easter Programs At Episcopal Churches

Fifth Annual Junior Art Show Opens April 20

John E. Metz To Wed Phoenix Girl

CHURCH NEWS

All Set For Good Time At Sedona

Was Honored By Pythian Sisters

Entertained At Bridge

Federated Women's Society

Easter Cantata At Federated Church

Mrs. Dodson New Head Tuba P.-T. A.

Use only one level teaspoonful

The Society, Church and Club News page of the *Coconino Sun* was often chatty and kept the community current on club meetings, engagements, school programs, charity events and more. *Courtesy of the* Daily Sun, *photographed by Flagstaff Public Library staff.*

and were reported along with wishes for a speedy recovery. It leaves one to wonder how the reporter received this information! Also notable were the well-documented travels of the town doctors. One had only to read the Personals to discover if Dr. Raymond was back from visiting his niece or Dr. Fronske had returned from the Grand Canyon.[12]

In fact, the whereabouts of almost every Flagstaff citizen in the '20s and '30s could be determined by thumbing through the *Sun*. Movements of the wealthy were tracked most diligently, followed by reports on the Old Guard, then the teachers, the business owners and the local ne'er-do-wells. Whether T.E. Pollock was in Kingman checking on livestock or T.A. Riordan was traveling in Europe, *Sun* readers were privy to this news. When John Doe was back in the local lockup for drunken conduct, everyone in town clicked their tongues. Out-of-town visitors were also duly noted, with the guest registers of the three largest hotels being printed at least every other week. All of this in addition to the parties and clubs mentioned previously kept neighbors informed on Flagstaff's social scene.

Page Two THE COCONIN

PERSONALS

Bill Cameron, son of Mr. and Mrs. Harold Cameron, has been ill with flu this week.

The son of J. R. Hickey, who is employed at Pilkington Motor Co., is seriously ill with pneumonia.

Chandler M. Wood, receiver of the Cady Lumber corporation, spent a day the first of this week at the main plant at McNary.

Joe Steinmetz has been kept at home by illness this week. Joe is employed in the printing department at Babbitts'.

J. D. Holt left Monday afternoon on a business trip to San Bernardino and Los Angeles and to visit his wife and sons in Pomona.

Joe Kerley, boss of the Kerley trading post at Tuba City, visited in Flagstaff Tuesday enroute from Tuba City to Albuquerque, where he is making headquarters this winter.

Charlie Isham, not to be outdone by his partner, Ted Spencer, who had been laid up with old-fashioned grip, himself took time out at home this week with similar miseries.

Columbus Giragi, co-publisher of The Sun, and Sam W. Proctor, connected with the state highway department, were here a short time Friday on the way from Phoenix to Holbrook.

The county board of supervisors held their regular monthly meeting Monday. Bob Thurston came from Williams, and the two Flagstaff members, Chairman Joe Tissaw and James D. Walkup, were on hand.

Next Tuesday and Wednesday the adjourned sessions of the annual Episcopal convocation will be held in Phoenix. Rev. and Mrs. S. S. Doron and children will attend, and it is believed there will be several others from Flagstaff.

State Senator Stauffer has introduced a bill to appropriate $8.70 to satisfy a claim of the Flagstaff Community Hotel Co. for refunds claimed due on distillate used in Hotel Monte Vista from December 29, 1926 to February 9, 1929.

A bill has been introduced by the judiciary committee of the state legislature to authorize the board of regents of the state university and the boards of education of the state teachers colleges

Tack Gaddis of Oak Creek was a Flagstaff visitor Saturday.

Wilmer Roberts, manager of the trading post at Jeddito, was in Flagstaff Tuesday.

Sonny Langston, son of Mr. and Mrs. Fred Langston, has been kept in by flu this week.

Earl Boyer of the Babbitt trading post at Tuba City was a visitor in town Tuesday.

Miss Winifred Lovell visited in Winslow last week-end with her sister, Miss Myrna Lovell.

Harold Longfellow is driving a new Chevrolet coach purchased this week from Pilkington Motor Co.

C. J. Babbitt and Herbert Babbitt returned Monday evening from a two day business trip to St. Johns.

Mr. and Mrs. R. B. Hazard and Miss Creta Bartlett of Tuba City were week-end visitors at Hotel Monte Vista.

Mr. and Mrs. Cecil E. Devaney returned Monday evening from Boulder dam, where they drove last Saturday.

Mr. and Mrs. Guy Longley spent last week-end in Clarkdale visiting Mrs. Longley's parents, Mr. and Mrs. John Sullivan.

Contractor and Mrs. Ole Solberg left Saturday for Grand Canyon, where Mr. Solberg will be employed for the next couple months.

Tommy, son of Mr. and Mrs. Joe D. Tissaw, has been ill with flu this week. Tommy is especially provoked as he has never before missed a day of school.

Superintendent M. R. Tillotson of Grand Canyon national park and J. E. Shirley, Fred Harvey transportation superintendent at Grand Canyon, spent part of Monday here.

T. E. Pollock, who is putting in most of the winter looking after his sheep and ranch interests in Chino valley and in the Phoenix country, spent part of this week at his offices here.

Persifor Fraser and young son of Philadelphia visited friends in Flagstaff Monday enroute to the Grand Canyon for a visit. The boy is a student at Arizona Desert school in Tucson.

Sam Richardson was here from Inscription House lodge Wednesday.

Miss Georgianna Isham has been kept home this week with flu, but is improving.

Sam Ashbrook, manager Hotel Monte Vista, has been ill with influenza this week.

John Metz has been an influenza sufferer this week and was forced to go home from his work Tuesday.

Dean, daughter of Mr. and Mrs. W. E. Jolly, has been ill this week with scarlet fever. She has a mild case.

Mr. and Mrs. E. J. Nordyke visited in Flagstaff Wednesday at the home of Dr. and Mrs. E. A. Miller.

Dan Molino, employed at Hotel Monte Vista, returned to work Wednesday after several days illness with flu.

Mr. and Mrs. Russell Miller of Tuba City visited Mrs. Miller's parents, Mr. and Mrs. Ed Easton, last week-end.

Mr. and Mrs. R. H. Simpson and son John Howard returned Monday evening from Phoenix, where they spent the week-end.

Leighton Cres motored to Phoenix with J. Morris Richards of the state education department. He will return home today.

Mrs. A. J. Mitchell has as guest Mrs. L. L. Wallace of Kingman. She was Mrs. Mitchell's guest at the Woman's club party.

Mrs. Leo F. Weaver and Miss Billie Weaver of Lees Ferry dude ranch were registered at the Hotel Monte Vista Monday and Tuesday.

Dr. H. L. Kilhoffer arrived from Phoenix the first part of the week for inspection of CCC camps. He will probably be located in this district several months.

J. R. Cooper, who has been at Hot Springs, N. M., two weeks, returned home last Thursday. He is feeling fine since taking the hot bath treatments there.

Dr. and Mrs. V. M. Slipher drove to Cornville Tuesday, where Mrs. Slipher will visit Mr. and Mrs. Frank Gyberg, while Dr. Slipher attends to business in Phoenix.

Carr Schwarz left this week for the coast where he will be gone a week or 10 days. Mrs. Schwarz has been visiting her parents there several weeks and he will join her.

Mr. and Mrs. Jack M. Wilson returned the first of the week from Phoenix, where they went last week to take home their little granddaughter, who had been here

R. H. Simpson returned Monday evening from Phoenix, where he spent the week-end.

Jim Edghill, who has been ill the past month or so, was taken to Mercy hospital Sunday.

Mr. and Mrs. J. C. Brown of the Gap trading post were Flagstaff visitors the first of the week.

Mrs. Mark MacIntosh will leave this morning with her husband and the college basketball team for Phoenix, where she will visit several days.

Mrs. K. J. Nackard and son Phillip returned Sunday evening from a buying trip to Los Angeles. They visited relatives in Indio, Calif., on the return trip.

Mrs. Agnes Samsky has been ill this week with flu. Her parents, Mr. and Mrs. Tom Fitzmorris of Congress Junction, were called here Monday evening.

Maurine Smith, daughter of Mr. and Mrs. A. W. Smith, who has been seriously ill with pneumonia, is getting along splendidly, well on the way to recovery.

Mr. and Mrs. Fred Henderson and Mr. and Mrs. Harold Huffer drove to Boulder dam last week-end to look at the giant structure, with which they were greatly impressed.

H. V. Watson returned Monday from Los Angeles, where he attended to business last week. He was called home by the illness of his daughter Edith, who has scarlet fever.

Mrs. Frank Quirk and her niece, Miss Harriet Paul, left Wednesday by car for Phoenix, where they are visiting Mrs. Quirk's sister, Mrs. Rose Garing. They plan to return this week-end.

John Francis, proprietor Bass Point resort, Mormon lake; George Atterbury and Stanton Borum, the latter of Leupp, are all at Agua Caliente hot springs resting up and taking the baths.

Mrs. C. E. Hablutzel, who ha[s] been seriously ill with influenz[a] this week, is able to be out of be[d] although still weak. Her littl[e] daughter Caroline has been stayin[g] with Mrs. Mark MacIntosh.

F. G. "Bake" Baker, who h[as] been employed in Babbitts' har[d]ware department, resigned th[is] week to become manager of t[he] Sprouse-Reitz store in Buckeye. [He] will probably leave this week-e[nd].

Horton Woodard, graduate [of] the college here and brother [of] Pete Woodard, at present a colle[ge] student here, is now employed [in] the classified advertising depa[rt]ment of the Arizona Republic

This example of the *Coconino Sun's* Personals page names residents suffering from the flu, scarlet fever and other contagious maladies. Other one- and two-sentence entries kept the community up to date on visitors, business deals and who's doing what around town. *Courtesy of the* Daily Sun, *photographed by Flagstaff Public Library staff.*

In 1946, the newspaper was renamed the *Arizona Daily Sun* and changed from a weekly to a daily paper. Platt Cline was the editor, and he remained with the newspaper in some capacity until his retirement in 1976. Cline was a beloved and respected figure in town; he helped fund NAU's Cline library, which is named in his honor. Cline was also a historian; he authored two books on Flagstaff that pay homage to the town and its founders and citizens.[13]

Today the *Daily Sun* is owned by Lee Enterprises and is published six days a week. Gone is the juicy gossip and salacious details that peppered the *Coconino Sun*. Even the detailed accounting of council meetings and city disputes has been toned down or cut altogether. One can't help but notice how less informed we are on civic matters and how *dry* the local news has become. However, as a psychiatrist I interviewed for the book pointed out, the *Sun* was not just an informative, benevolent presence in town. In the first half of the twentieth century it functioned a bit like Facebook does today. Whether you were "liked" or valued was reflected in its pages and in how often your name appeared within them. Some, like Marie Walkup, who was seldom mentioned, might have felt shamed or invisible; others might have chafed at their lack of privacy. Like so many influences it was a mixed bag at best. Perhaps the paper's greatest value is in the retrospective view it gives of the town today.

4

THE EARLY 1920s

How, when and where JD and Thelma Marie met is difficult to determine and depends on the source of the information. The *Arizona Republic* wrote that the couple met while he was working at the Museum of Northern Arizona, Dr. Harold Colton's establishment. That would be incorrect, as the museum was not even established until well after the couple were married. JD's 1972 obituary states that he was "initially employed by Babbitt Brothers" when he arrived in Flagstaff, and that corresponds with what little is known about his life until 1924. Marie Green was said to have clerked at the Babbitt stores, although no dates of employment were given. It's most likely that the couple met through work. Their wedding announcement in June 1925 said that the newlyweds had lived in town "for several years where they were popular members of the Babbitt organization."[14]

Eighteen months before their marriage, JD Walkup's name began to appear with some regularity in the pages of the *Sun*. It seems this tall, handsome bachelor, a decorated veteran from World War I, was finally being noticed. JD was to become a leader among the wave of hopeful newcomers settling the area. One of the first mentions of him is found on the front page of the May 16, 1924 issue of the paper. He and several other men made the round-trip trek to Rainbow National Bridge by automobile in only three days, taking a new route that cut toward Navajo Mountain. They reported on their progress—road conditions, hazards, et cetera—to the *Sun*, which printed their observations in some detail. The group found

Babbitts Backcountry building is part of the original 1888 Babbitt Brothers store and occupies a corner of downtown Flagstaff. JD Walkup began clerking for Babbitt Brothers when he first arrived in town. *Author's collection.*

the new road far superior to the older trail, which went through Kayenta and took two weeks longer. A decade later, JD would apply his political muscle to creating and paving roads in Coconino County, ensuring the area was easily accessible to tourists.

As local baseball heated up that summer, Babbitt Brothers joined the craze and formed a team, the Cannibals. JD was on the roster, initially at second base then later in the season as shortstop. After losing their first game, the Cannibals buckled down and were victorious in the next four. The team continued on a roll and began to draw a good-size crowd of fans and spectators. The Cannibals were known as a raucous lot, disputing "bad calls" and generally unrepentant to pleas for sportsmanship. They ended the season with a fizzle in September with several losses and a no-show on the twenty-eighth in Seligman. The newspaper gently razed them, but as with the other teams, it all made for good baseball.[15]

When JD was not working and playing ball that summer, he found time for other amusements. He was among a group of locals who attended several

THE NAVAJO SQUAW DANCE

The Squaw Dance was one of several ceremonial dances held annually on reservation land that non-Native people were allowed to watch. In 1924, the dance was held near Cameron and attracted over five hundred Navajos accompanied by livestock and horses. It was a festive event, with the Navajo women decked out in silver and turquoise jewelry and each tribesperson carrying their own blanket. The event lasted several days and included gambling and swapping between the Native Americans and a much-anticipated horse race after the dance. During all of the festivities, the white spectators were relegated to the perimeter.

The dance itself was at night near a large bonfire and was preceded by the Sick Song. This two-hour singing ritual was performed by Navajo men and centered on a hogan made from cottonwood branches laid against a log framework of the same material. Inside the hogan were three very ill Native Americans who would hopefully find healing from the ceremony. As the ritual began, the medicine men and Navajo warriors gathered outside the structure and began to chant, seamlessly alternating their songs. Several clans were represented, and it was said that the blending of the voices and matching incantations was mesmerizing.

After the Sick Song and a short distance from the hogan, a circle of men and women began to form around a large bonfire. The group was mainly composed of Navajo braves interspersed with the white spectators. The dance began when the appointed Navajo woman, decked out in feathers, advanced to the center of the circle. The men once again provided the vocalizations, their chants creating the music of the dance. The lone woman started to move about the circle, eyeing the braves up and down until she decided on a partner. Gliding gracefully, she grabbed him by the back of his shirt and began to dance backward, spinning the hapless male around toward her while keeping a firm grip on the shirt. After that the other women joined in, and soon there was a flurry of galloping, rhythmic stomping, all done to the rich vocalizations of the men who performed earlier. Occasionally one of the young women would go into the ring of white spectators to select a partner, spinning the man until he paid her with some coin.*

* *Coconino Sun*, June 27, 1924.

of the popular Indian Dances, which were held on the reservation. The Navajo Squaw Dance took place in June on a low mesa near the Cameron bridge. Both the dance's name and colorful reporting would be considered offensive today, but it was widely attended back then by Navajo and Hopi tribes. Many of the Native Americans traveled one hundred or more miles to participate. The Hopi Snake Dance was even more popular, drawing a record-breaking two thousand non-Native observers in 1922.

Both the Squaw Dance and the Snake Dance were highly regarded ceremonies that drew observers from all over the world. The non-Natives were mostly respectful, although occasionally a tourist would try to snap a forbidden photo. When that occurred the tribal police would deal swiftly with the offender, keeping the event peaceful. The tribes managed to keep these incredible dances open to the public for decades, which benefited both cultures. JD Walkup was noted as attending many of the ceremonies in subsequent years, which may have contributed to his enthusiasm at promoting the All-Indian Powwow.[16]

By the mid-1920s, the townspeople had joined with elected officials in realizing and accepting tourism as a huge source of revenue to be tapped. Much of Flagstaff's good fortune was, and is, due to its geography. The town is located about ninety miles south of the Grand Canyon and twenty miles north of Sedona and is surrounded by Navajo and Hopi Reservations. Flagstaff sits at roughly 7,000 feet and is nestled into the base of Mount Humphries, which tops out at 12,633 feet. The climate is still touted as ideal for every season. There's skiing in the winter, hiking and mushroom hunting in the fall and sunny summer days with cool clear nights to enjoy. The famed Western author Zane Gray visited regularly and often stayed with his entourage at the Weatherford Hotel. He sang Flagstaff's glories whenever he could and pressed the town fathers to secure adequate water resources for the future boom in tourism.[17]

Major movie companies who specialized in producing the popular Westerns of the day had come to rely on men like Allen Doyle to procure enough horses and authentic Native American "extras" for their films. Doyle could round up all that was needed with little notice, which made Flagstaff a popular town with the studios. While the actual filming usually took place sixty miles east on the reservation or south in Sedona, the shoot would begin staging in town. The Hotel Monte Vista, built in 1926, became the hub of activity for many of these endeavors as well as for city business and tourism.[18]

The railroad continued to play an important part in the town's daily life, transporting visitors and merchandise along its tracks. However, Route 66,

THE HOPI SNAKE DANCE

The Hopi Snake Dance was usually held in August and was easily the most popular of the tribal dances among the non-Natives. The date of the dance could vary and was well-publicized in advance, with pleas to the public for any large snakes. The Hopis were known to pay for rattlers and bull snakes as the number of snakes required for the ceremony was substantial. In essence, the Snake Dance was held to petition the gods for enough rain in the coming year to insure good crops. However, tribal members could also relay a secret wish during the dance, which the snakes would then carry to the gods when they were finally released.

While the public's help in gathering snakes was solicited, tradition dictated that some snakes be obtained from each of the four directions in the days preceding the dance. After being washed and purified, the reptiles were kept in a corn husk enclosure guarded by select tribesmen. In separate kivas, the various clan members spent several days fasting and preparing for the sacred ritual that was to come. On the afternoon of the dance the spectators gathered in the arena,

This graphic photograph of a Hopi man with a large snake in his mouth was taken circa 1924 and was likely related to the Hopi Snake Dance ritual. *Library of Congress Online Catalog, Hopi Indian Study no. 28.*

some keeping their seats for hours to ensure a good position from which to experience the incredible event. It began when members of the Snake Fraternity emerged from their kiva, chanting and dancing their way to the enclosure. The snakes were then quickly picked up by the dancers and carried into the arena. Snakes could be placed by a dancer inside his mouth or gathered up and held like a bouquet. An occasional snake was released and encouraged to depart toward one of the four corners. The Snake Fraternity continued dancing and chanting while handling the snakes until the end of the ritual, when they gathered in a circle and threw the snakes into a pile. Then immediately the performers picked up the snakes and ran off with them, taking them to all four directions of the earth.

The excitement of the dance was a crowd-pleaser, although an occasional spectator would become unruly and kick dirt at the snakes. When that happened, it was said that the Hopi would allow a snake to come close to the crowd before retrieving it, thus frightening the observers into minding their manners.*

* *Coconino Sun*, August 22, 1924, 1.

which ran through the south side of town, now carried the city's dreams for the future. People driving the Mother Road would stay a few nights in one of the newly sprouted motels along the way, visiting the Grand Canyon or Sedona before continuing westward to California. The opportunities that came with the automobile were available to both travelers and towns alike, and Flagstaff was quick to seize the moment.

As the town continued to aggressively market its assets a new breed of citizenry was making itself known. JD Walkup was part of that crowd, and his name began to find its way into the *Sun* outside of baseball games and dances. The young transplant was working for Babbitt Brothers, and he was beginning to participate in community life. A blurb in the October 17, 1924 *Sun* noted that while most of the locals had shot their bucks, JD took his down with a knife. In December he made his first appearance on the society page as a guest of Mrs. HC Metz's "attractively appointed Christmas party." The partygoers attended a play at the Normal School and then proceeded to Mrs. Metz's for dinner and a game of five hundred. The party was in honor of four Flagstaff teachers, but there's no indication of who invited JD as a guest.[19]

Looking north up San Francisco Street, circa 1943. The Hotel Monte Vista is on the right, midway up the photo. *Library of Congress online catalogue, photographer Jack Delano.*

Walkup started 1925 with a bold move when he and several other young men chartered the Mathian Club. According to the *Sun*, *Mathian* means good fellowship; it is also Hebrew for the "gift of gab." There were five charter members, with seven more voted in at the second meeting held in January. Several of the men roomed at the house where the club was headquartered, and a housekeeper was hired to provide meals. JD was appointed acting president, but after January news about the Mathians was scant.[20] The very next week Walkup made the front page again, this time when he was formally installed as commander of the local Howitzer Company. JD, a first lieutenant, took this post command seriously and it was said that he would bring the organization "up to the highest possible point of efficiency." With a demanding job, a post command and a newly formed club to lead, JD Walkup had a full plate in January 1925. Although it might have appeared daunting to outsiders, it foreshadowed the busy civic life that he seemed to relish a decade later.[21]

JD's time as the commander of the Howitzer Company proved to be short-lived. As he became more deeply involved with his career at Babbitt

Brothers he was sent to a trading post in Kingman, a town 180 miles west of Flagstaff. No matter whether he drove, took the train or a combination of both, it would have been a tedious journey. A blurb on the Local Brevities page at the end of February noted that JD had come into town from Kingman and dropped by to visit friends.[22] He was in town almost monthly after that, until it was noted in mid-April that Walkup would be the manager of Babbitt's Cibicue Trading Post. Somewhere in that time frame he had started seeing Thelma Marie Green, but there is no mention of them as a couple in the paper.

Speaking of Thelma Marie, what do we know about her young life during these years? In a word, nothing. Her name is not mentioned as attending any of the teas, parties or social clubs during the early 1920s. If she attended any of the Snake Dances or ceremonials on the reservation, her name was not printed along with all the others who did. She would have been eighteen in 1923, finished with high school and possibly working. The *Coconino Sun* reported that Marie had lived for some time with the T.E. Pollock family in Flagstaff. Pollock was arguably the wealthiest and most powerful man in town at that time. He owned the local bank and had cattle and land interests scattered throughout northern Arizona. His wife Mary was very active in the community and at the Normal School, and both of their comings and goings were duly noted. The Pollocks had two young children, a boy and girl, and it's possible Marie helped with the children. That, however, is pure conjecture. There's no mention of Marie in association with the Pollocks or anyone else in the gossipy sections of the *Sun*. In fact, the first mention found regarding Thelma Marie Green was the announcement of her marriage to James Douglas Walkup on June 15, 1925.[23]

5

THE START OF A FAMILY

The wedding announcement was printed in the June 19, 1925 *Coconino Sun*. Under the bolded heading "J.D. Walkup and Miss Marie Green Married," it read:

> *Miss Marie Green and James D. Walkup were married at 11 o'clock Monday morning at the Federated parsonage by Rev. H.F. Softley in the presence of Miss Alice Brown and Tillman Hendricks, who acted as bridesmaid and best man. They left on the early afternoon train for Holbrook, from there going to Cibicue on the White River Indian reservation, where Mr. Walkup is manager of the Cibicue Indian trading post for Babbitt Bros. Both Mr. and Mrs. Walkup lived in Flagstaff for several years, where they were popular members of the Babbitt organization.*[24]

After the ceremony, the newlyweds took the train ninety miles due east to the rough-and-tumble railroad town of Holbrook. The area had been a real Cowtown until a few years before, boasting one of the largest cattle ranches in the United States when it was known as a haven for rustlers. Although the Babbitt brothers had bought much of the acreage in 1902, Holbrook was still known as a tough town. The Walkups would not have lingered but would have made their way south another ninety miles to the Cibicue trading post, where they would live for the next fifteen months.

The roads available in 1925 from Holbrook to Cibicue were little more than foot trails in some places. Whether the newlyweds traveled by cart or

It's difficult to capture the beauty and isolation of Cibicue, a census designated place on the Fort Apache Indian Reservation. JD and Marie lived here for approximately sixteen months after marrying. *Author's collection.*

As nearly as I can tell from my research, this deserted building in Cibicue, Arizona, sits exactly where the old trading post was located in 1925. *Author's collection.*

TRADING POSTS

The establishment of Indian trading posts in northern Arizona began in the 1860s. Outposts had sprung up decades earlier in the East along rivers and mountain passes. In the western territories the rough terrain, changing elevations and uncharted desert delayed their appearance. Kit Carson's Mountain Men were among the first to start informal trading with the goods carried in their saddlebags. The trade business solidified and grew exponentially with improved trails, reliable river crossings and the coming of the railroad. Soon trading posts were sprouting up at convenient locations for the individual tribes. To be efficient and profitable, the posts needed to be located as close as possible to good roads or the rails. Babbitt Brothers owned a number of posts in the northlands, but other stores stayed in a family for generations. The Hubbels, Lees and McGees were well-known families who ran outposts and were respected in Arizona for being fair in their dealings with the Navajo.

In the early 1900s, a trusted post manager was much more than a white trader at the store. He also acted as banker and barterer and, if proven trustworthy, occupied a position of honor among the tribe. He was often asked to mediate minor disputes between neighbors and might have recommended and administered medications to the Native Americans if they were ill. The trader was also the intermediary between the lawmakers in Washington and the tribe he served. This meant keeping abreast of the ever-changing rules and regulations and interpreting them to the community.

For the family operating the post, life could be very isolated. Reservation land was often remote and difficult to get to. The trader's children were often sent away for schooling; those who stayed became proficient in the Native language and lived a life far different from their white peers.

In an article from the 1939 Southwest All-Indian Powwow souvenir program entitled "Navajo Indian Traders," the following was written: "An old-time Indian trader was asked his description of a trader's functions among the Navajo. After considerable thought he replied, 'He brings them into the world, feeds and clothes them while they live and buries them when they die.'"

While not all traders were so honest and respected, nor all tribes so welcoming to a white interloper, those who forged a good relationship with the community they served lived a unique and fascinating life. It's notable that by the 1930s some Native American families had taken over managing the trading posts themselves.*

* The Flagstaff Public Library has, as of February 2021, an excellent online exhibit of pamphlets, videos and other memorabilia from past Southwest All-Indian Powwows that were held in Flagstaff. The information on the trading posts was found in a souvenir program from July 1939 on page 23 in an article titled "Navajo Indian Traders." NAU Special Collections also has access to amazing stories and pictures from the annual event, and the Powwow is certainly worthy of a book of its own.

car—or even horseback—is not known. The population of Cibicue today is only 1,700; it was slightly less 90 years ago. The landscape remains stark and lonely but is majestic in its solitude. The colorful, spiraling mesas that surround the settlement frame the desert floor with its patches of grass. The area is hilly and the Apache still tend livestock and keep horses on their land.[25]

Life on a trading post would have been what you made of it. The cultural differences in a place only ninety miles from rough-and-tumble Holbrook were extreme and even more pronounced when compared to Flagstaff. As a rule, white people were treated with suspicion and aloofness by the Native Americans until some kind of trust was established. Since the Walkups lived there only a little over a year, it's hard to say what their experience was like.

The Walkups ventured into Flagstaff on business at least once in February 1926. When JD returned to Cibicue, Marie stayed in town for a week afterward with Alice Brown.[26] Alice and Marie had been good friends and years later Alice helped Marie with the children. By that time Alice was married to John Weston, another local man who once worked for Babbitt Brothers. Alice Weston was known to the Walkup children as La La and, according to the *Sun*, mother and children adored her.

In September 1926, the Walkups returned to Flagstaff to live. Marie would have been five months into her first pregnancy and perhaps the remoteness of the reservation worried her. The town they returned to was ever expanding with an eye toward tourism and would incorporate in 1928. It adopted a new slogan that summer: "Flagstaff—Where Winter Plays with Summer" submitted by a contestant from the Teacher's College. The newly

A 1959 aerial view of the Flagstaff Country Club's golf course. The clubhouse is hidden in a clump of trees on the left. *With permission of Northern Arizona University Special Collections–Cline Library; Faure, Andre collection.*

formed Flagstaff golf club garnered its share of attention, hoping to appeal to the town's upper crust and those ever-lucrative tourist dollars. The Hotel Monte Vista was finally under construction and promised to be thoroughly modern with all the latest amenities, such as indoor plumbing and electricity. JD would have an office in the Monte V a decade later, but for now the couple rented a home on North Leroux and JD began driving a delivery truck for Frank Brooks.[27]

Daniel Green Walkup was born on January 5, 1927, two days after his father's twenty-eighth birthday. The blurb in the January 7, 1927 *Sun* read: "Jim Walkup, who drives Frank Brooks' delivery wagon, didn't really know if he was coming or going Wednesday for before he knew it he repeatedly drove right back to the hospital where Mrs. Walkup and that fine seven-pound boy are staying. Daniel Green is the young chap's name and he weighed seven pounds when he checked in at 4 a.m."

The small family remained in the Leroux home that year, but it was not an easy time for them. It appears that JD severed ties with Babbitt Brothers when he and Marie returned in September. The man he was driving for, Frank Brooks, was a popular local businessman who dealt in groceries and the like.

The Flagstaff Country Club

Almost forgotten save for a handful of locals is the gently rolling, dirt-packed acreage that was once the Flagstaff Country Club and nine-hole golf course. For the past three decades the area has been carved into trails and jumps by local mountain bikers who speed along the paths while oblivious to the history of the land on which they ride.

Located about four miles north of downtown, the site was chosen in 1925 after a brief search by a few influential men who had wisely recruited Tim Riordan's assistance in the search. Riordan knew a thing or two about golfing; the Riordan estate sported a three-hole course, each with three different approaches. When the idea of designing a town golf course and club house turned serious, he helped evaluate several possibilities before the group landed on the parcel east of the old reservoir. The fairways would be dirt-packed, with nature kept in check by daily grooming with mowers. In 1926, it was decided that the greens would actually be large ovals defined by cottonseed oil. Hand-operated rollers were kept at each hole, and it was the individual golfers' responsibility to roll down the area for the next player after completing their putt.

Work on the nine-hole course began in March 1925 and was completed by late May. The decision was made to build the clubhouse the following year, although that project was delayed until the 1930s. Regardless, memberships sold rapidly and a resolution was passed that capped the roster at seventy-five. The early initiation fee was thirty-five dollars, saving charter members fifteen dollars. Yearly dues were twenty dollars. Provisions were made for out-of-towners—fifty cents a day—and some exceptions were made for ladies.

Golfing proved to be popular with both sexes and all summer long locals and visitors could be found at the club. A pro was hired the second year to tweak the course and provide helpful tips to members, and soon tournaments and leagues were part of Flagstaff's social scene. Silver cups, gift certificates and other small prizes were donated by local merchants to add an air of fun and legitimacy to the mix. When the country club clubhouse was finally erected, it was a large, attractive building made of stone and replete with a restaurant, bar and large dance floor.

In 2021, there are still some locals who remember traipsing up and down the fairways, carrying golf bags for the duffers who played there regularly. One former caddy walked the course while reminiscing about the days in the 1960s when the country club was the place to be. "You wouldn't know it now," he said with a smile, "but this was the seat of power in Flagstaff those years. And it was a gorgeous golf course—exciting too. Many a deal was made on these fairways or in the clubhouse bar. More than once the caddies were told to keep their mouths shut about what we heard."

Sometime in the mid-1970s a new country club was built on the east side of town. It's still in play today, with spectacular views and a well-manicured eighteen-hole course. For some locals, though, it will never come close to the dirt-packed fairways and cottonseed-oiled greens of the original.*

* Information on the formation of the Flagstaff Country Club was found in multiple issues of the Sun that spanned the years 1924 to 1927 and beyond. It was a project that was debated and delayed until 1925. I was also fortunate enough to have several conversations with longtime Flagstaff residents who had wonderful memories of the town's first country club and all that transpired, on the green and off.

The first quarter of 1927, JD continued to work for Brooks as well as taking an odd job here and there. All this time, though, he was working on a business idea of his own that he unveiled in May. A headline on the front page of the May 20 *Coconino Sun* trumpeted: "Walkup to Open Soft Drink Factory."

JD had decided to go head-to-head with his employer Frank Brooks who—along with all his other enterprises—was the proprietor of Skylight City Bottling Works. To get some idea of how this played out locally, a few weeks prior the *Sun* ran one of its business-friendly "puff" articles on the front page. Under the headline "Flagstaff's Water Is Basis for Local Bottling Industry," the item read in part:

> *Do you know we have an industry in Flagstaff which is based on its being able to secure absolutely pure and fresh water? It's a fact and the industry is that of beverage making, operated by Frank Brooks on West Railroad avenue. Mr. Brooks holds franchises on several nationally known drinks, the best known being Coco Cola. His franchise entitles him to manufacture and sell in Coconino and Yavapai counties. Besides Coco Cola, Mr. Brooks*

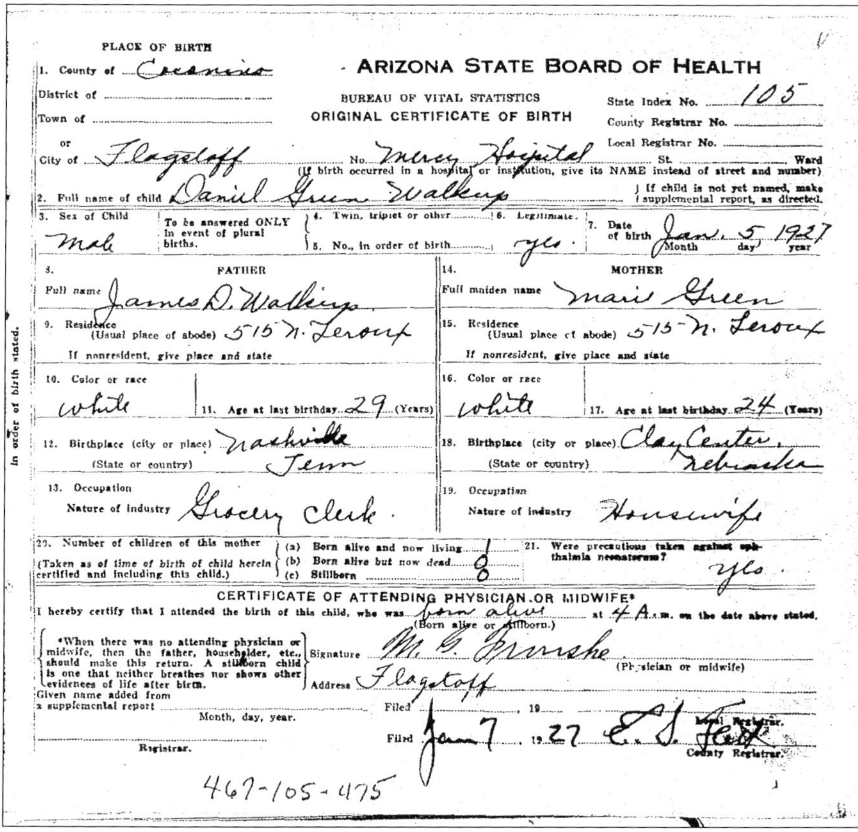

PLACE OF BIRTH

1. County of Coconino

District of

Town of

or

City of Flagstaff No. Mercy Hospital St. Ward

(If birth occurred in a hospital or institution, give its NAME instead of street and number)

ARIZONA STATE BOARD OF HEALTH

BUREAU OF VITAL STATISTICS

ORIGINAL CERTIFICATE OF BIRTH

State Index No. 105

County Registrar No.

Local Registrar No.

2. Full name of child Daniel Green Walkup (If child is not yet named, make supplemental report, as directed.)

3. Sex of Child: male | To be answered ONLY in event of plural births. 4. Twin, triplet or other | 5. No., in order of birth | 6. Legitimate: yes | 7. Date of birth Jan. 5, 1927 (Month, day, year)

8. FATHER	14. MOTHER
Full name James D. Walkup	Full maiden name Marie Green
9. Residence (Usual place of abode) 515 N. Leroux. If nonresident, give place and state	15. Residence (Usual place of abode) 515 N. Leroux. If nonresident, give place and state
10. Color or race: white. 11. Age at last birthday 29 (Years)	16. Color or race: white. 17. Age at last birthday 24 (Years)
12. Birthplace (city or place) Nashville (State or country) Tenn	18. Birthplace (city or place) Clay Center, (State or country) Nebraska
13. Occupation, Nature of industry Grocery Clerk.	19. Occupation, Nature of industry Housewife

20. Number of children of this mother (Taken as of time of birth of child herein certified and including this child.) (a) Born alive and now living 1 (b) Born alive but now dead 0 (c) Stillborn 0

21. Were precautions taken against ophthalmia neonatorum? yes.

CERTIFICATE OF ATTENDING PHYSICIAN OR MIDWIFE*

I hereby certify that I attended the birth of this child, who was born alive (Born alive or stillborn.) at 4 A. m. on the date above stated.

*When there was no attending physician or midwife, then the father, householder, etc., should make this return. A stillborn child is one that neither breathes nor shows other evidences of life after birth.

Signature M. G. Fronske (Physician or midwife)

Address Flagstaff

Given name added from a supplemental report .... Month, day, year. .... Registrar.

Filed .... 19.... Local Registrar.

Filed Jan 7 1927 E. S. [illegible] County Registrar.

467-105-475

The Walkup's firstborn, Daniel Green Walkup, entered the world just a few days after his father's twenty-eighth birthday. Notice JD's occupation is listed as Grocery Clerk. *Courtesy K. Renner.*

> *has contracts for the manufacture of Delaware Punch, Hires Root Beer, and Orange, Lemon and Lime crushes.... The Brooks Bottling Works is a model plant. Although its capacity is small, yet for the first four months of this year it has turned out 1,600 cases of drinks with 48 bottles to the case.*[28]

Following is an excerpt from the May 20 article a few weeks later:

> *Flagstaff will within a few weeks have another soft drink bottling works, machinery for it now being in transit. The managing partner will be Jim Walkup, well known here through several years residence in this section, part of which time he worked for Frank E. Brooks, proprietor of the successful Skylight City Bottling works, probably the largest and best equipped of*

> *its kind in the southwest. Jim when this was written hadn't settled upon a location, but it is likely will be in the basement of the Masonic Temple, in the flour mill building, or, perhaps in the commissary building at the Cady Lumber corporation sawmill....Mr. Walkup says he has franchises for bottling several soft drinks and that he expects to get more. Of course, in addition, he expects to manufacture pop in all flavors....The name of the new competing concern, it is understood, will be Flagstaff Bottling Works.*

We can safely assume JD had severed ties with Brooks or vice-versa. Not surprisingly, it appears the competition with his former employee caused Brooks some consternation. There was an uptick in advertisements for his products on the Local Brevities page. "Brooks Bottling Works for those delicious summer drinks" and "Hires Root Beer in bottles, good for the spring fever" appeared regularly in the *Sun*. However, Brooks need not have been overly concerned; there is no mention of the Flagstaff Bottling Works after May 20 in either the paper or as a registered business. On June 10, the

The family was living in this house on North Agassiz Street when Rose Marie was born on August 24, 1929. JD's occupation is listed as "Hardware Clerk" on Rose's birth certificate. *Courtesy K. Renner.*

paper noted JD had spent time in Phoenix on business and then returned home and was "helping in Switzer's Hardware store." One sentence on the front page of the July 29, 1927 *Sun* read: "JD Walkup returned from Kingman and is clerking with Switzer Hardware store."

JD stayed with Switzer's for several years. The family moved about a block east to 510 North Agassiz Street before the birth of their second child, Rose Marie, in 1929. The *Sun* took notice and ran the following sentence: "Jim Walkup of Switzer's Hardware wears a smile several degrees wider and more infectious than in a long time, induced by joy over the birth at Mercy Hospital Sunday night of a pretty little girl, whose little brother says he doesn't know but what she may be better than a brother after all."

Baby Rose was born at 5:15 p.m. on August 24, 1929, and like her brother Daniel, was delivered by Dr. Fronske. While it was a happy occasion a sense of foreboding must have colored JD's outlook when he considered his family's economic situation. The Great Depression was already playing havoc in some of the eastern states, and soon Flagstaff would feel its effects. The coming years were dark and would test the town's character and alter its economic base as the whole nation grappled with the crisis.

6

THE DEPRESSION YEARS

Flagstaff suffered less than most towns its size during the Great Depression, but the town was affected nonetheless. The lumber mills had been Flagstaff's economic backbone for the past four decades and had provided steady employment for many men. This all changed in the 1930s when demand for processed wood decreased and businesses the mill had supplied closed. While the mills would eventually reopen, production never rallied. Tourism also declined rapidly and the many motels and hotels that had sprouted in the mid-1920s were left with empty rooms. Unlike the lumber business, the tourist industry did rebound in relatively few years and remains vital even today.[29]

Sometime in 1930 or '31, Walkup went in search of a position more stable than the one at Switzer's Hardware. He found it a few miles north of town on Coyote Range, the ranch owned by Dr. Harold Colton and his wife, Mary-Russell. Exactly what JD's position was at the ranch is unknown—or perhaps it's more accurate to say it depends on what source one finds. The couple's third child, John Samuel, was born while the family was living at Coyote Range. On the baby's January 6, 1933 birth certificate, father's occupation was listed as "Ranch Over-seer." The following year, an article in the *Sun* endorsing Walkup for county supervisor read in part, "For the last several years he [JD] has been mechanical and ranch superintendent for Dr. Harold S. Colton."[30] No detailed description of Walkup's duties was found in Dr. Colton's extensive diaries, although JD's name was found

The Colton property was extensive and included the Museum of Northern Arizona and what is now known as the Colton Research Center. The buildings pictured here are close to where Coyote Range was located. *Author's collection.*

in Colton's telephone directory from 1933. Written by hand, the entry read: "JDW F 12R3."[31]

At some point during the early 1930s, Flagstaff began emerging from the Depression. The town was certainly helped by the infusion of cash for highway maintenance and unemployment. Over at Coyote Range, Walkup had turned his attention toward civic matters and politics. Much like his employer Dr. Colton, he had become a "joiner." During those years, JD served as president of the Flagstaff Game Protective Association. He was a master of the local Masonic Lodge and a commander at the local American Legion post. Walkup was also a member of the Knights of Pythias. The order had an auxiliary group for women, the Pythian Sisters, but from all accounts, Marie was never a member.[32]

In 1934, JD Walkup decided to run for county supervisor of district one. At age thirty-five it was his first campaign for public office, and he ran as a Democrat. He received a wide majority of votes in the primary and in November 1934, won the endorsement of the *Coconino Sun*. Under the

The Coltons

Dr. Harold Colton, a zoologist, and his wife Mary-Russell, a renown Philadelphia artist, lived on Coyote Range while overseeing the creation of the Museum of Northern Arizona. The Coltons had summered in Flagstaff many times before deciding to move here permanently in 1926. They were impressed by both the geographic beauty of the area and the scientific community that was developing around it. They bought some of the land owned by Flagstaff's first settler, Thomas McMillian, and built Coyote Range. It's said that their small estate was named for a pack of wild coyotes who roamed the area. Situated three miles north of town, the compound expanded to include buildings used as laboratories, studios, guesthouses and a barn. When a fire in 1928 destroyed the Coltons' beloved Malapais Manor, they rebuilt it the next year. The Colton House still stands today and can be reserved for weddings and retreats.

While the Coltons were active in civic and social affairs, they are best remembered for their tireless work solidifying the reputation of the Museum of Northern Arizona. The building is situated across Fort Valley Road from Coyote Range and was built circa 1935. The institute is world renowned for its artifacts and studies on the Colorado Plateau and has conducted many well-regarded research projects throughout the decades. While Dr. Colton represented the scientific community, Mary-Russell ensured that Native American art and culture would live on in the collected works at the museum. Both Coltons were highly regarded in Flagstaff and, indeed, throughout the Southwest.*

* I used several sources for the information on Harrold and Mary-Russell Ferrell Colton, including Cline, *Mountain Town*; Magnum and Magnum, *Flagstaff Past & Present*; and general information found from brochures that the Museum of Northern Arizona had available.

headline "Jim Walkup Well Fitted for Job as Co. Supervisor," the article read in part:

> *There are not many men in Coconino County better known than Mr. Walkup, who in the nearly 12 years he has lived here has taken an active, constructive part in public affairs....Jim was born in Nashville,*

> *Tenn., in 1899. After his school days, during which he secured a good education, he became connected with the Keith-Simmons Hardware Co. of Nashville. The war came on and Jim went overseas with the 30th division. He was in six major battles in Belgium and France....After the war he came west to regain his health, especially to recover from the effects of the gas....Mr. Walkup married Miss Marie Green here and they have three children, two of whom attend the college training school....This is the first time Mr. Walkup has run for public office. He is well-educated, intelligent, and an active, hard-working man, who puts his heart and soul into whatever job he has to do. One hundred per cent for this city and county and state, if elected he may be depended upon to give the duties of the office honest, careful and intelligent attention.*[33]

JD was elected by a healthy margin and would take office the following January.

7

THE GOOD YEARS

The mid-1930s were golden years for both JD Walkup and the town he represented. Flagstaff regained its aura of hustle and bustle as the tourists and conventioneers returned, and soon business was booming. The lumber mills reopened, and while they never regained the prominence they held before the Depression, they provided employment for a number of people. Hollywood once again came knocking and Lee Doyle was there to answer, rounding up the horses and movie extras the studios sought as well as providing a bridge to the reservation. Northern Arizona Normal School officially became Arizona State Teachers College at Flagstaff in 1929 and managed to weather the Depression better than it did World War II a decade later. Lowell Observatory would probably have suffered more during the Depression if astronomer Clyde Tombaugh hadn't discovered the planet Pluto in 1930. However, Tombaugh prevailed, and the Observatory maintained its prestige, attracting funding and academia outside of Arizona. All said, the town was back on its feet and looking toward a bright future when JD Walkup was sworn in as county supervisor of district one in January 1935.[34]

The newly installed official set to work and immediately created controversy at the board's first meeting in January. Disagreement arose over the reappointment of the county engineer, Major J.B. Wright. Major Wright's work had been deemed too expensive and he was widely assumed to be on the way out. This issue was old business, and action to void the major's contract should have been routine. However, JD moved that Wright keep his

TANGLE OVER CONTINUED EMPLOYMENT ENGINEER SUPERVISORS' PROBLEM

Board Two To One Against Reappointment Of Major Wright—Local Delegation Gets A Month's Stay

Belief that Major J. B. Wright, county engineer, was slated for removal by the new county board of supervisors provoked intense interest in the board's organization meeting Wednesday morning and was the inspiration of much oratory by local taxpayers intent on the major's reappointment.

The question came up immediately after the new board had elected Mr. Tissaw chairman and reappointed Clerk George A. Fleming, and began when Member James Walkup moved Major Wright's reappointment, and it developed that neither Chairman Tissaw nor Member Thurston were favorable. There were about 20 representative Flagstaff taxpayers ready and willing to take up the cudgel for the major, and reinforcing them there was a petition containing nearly 300 signatures asking his reappointment.

Throughout, the discussion was notable for the utter absence of any display of anger or ill feeling.

It finally was decided, upon motion of Member Walkup and amendment of Member Thurston to keep Major Wright on the job another month, the question of the economy or extravagance of his past work to be settled by study of the official files by a committee of nine taxpayers, three to be named by each member of the board. This committee is subject to the call of the supervisors.

Major Wright's salary from the county is $3000 a year. It was proposed to substitute for him two road foremen. While it was not announced at the meeting, one foremanship, in event of Wright's removal, was to go to W. H. Lockridge, of Anita, a surveyor and long time resident of this county.

Earl C. Slipher had been chosen to open the Wright affirmative, and pointed out that with some $60,000 a year to be expended in highway department it was urgent that a competent engineer be kept in charge; otherwise as much or more than his salary would have to be paid for special engineering

(Continued on Page Eight)

Celebrated His 77th Birthday On New Year's Day

T. A. Riordan, for whom it was decided more than 77 years ago that it would be easier for him to direct his accounting and coordinate all his business and social affairs if his natal day was the first of the year, received many congratulations from friends here and elsewhere Tuesday, in connection with the double event. He and Mrs. Riordan had a pleasant time on his 77th birthday, which was ushered in as have been all his birthdays, with ringing of bells, sounding of whistles, and other noises of revelry. Before the day ended he was trying to figure out whether three of his friends had ganged up on him, or whether it was pure coincidence. He received combined birthday and New Year telegrams from John Hitchcock, manager Santa Fe railway coast lines, James Duffy, Santa Fe traffic manager, and Victor Patrosso, manager El Tovar hotel at Grand Canyon, none of whom he thought knew January 1 was his birthday. Mr. Riordan and Dr. E. S. Miller of this city, now in Phoenix, whose birth were on the same day and year, exchanged felicitations.

Two Long Valley Road Sectors Are Being Constructed

Clearing has started on two sec-

To Widen Na Oak Creek

The Skoussen brothe ors, are moving men ment into Oak Creek construct the Sedona road into a new and way southeast from first sector to be ed is about four running from Grassho just west of Dry cre under supervision of t eau of public roads. most all new constr survey calls for cutti possible curves. It is the new road will be or the same as that Gardens to the top hill.

CADY LU SALE SE TO JANU

Death Of Mr. Delayed Co Biddin

Sale of the Cady poration property, have been made at Flagstaff, Monday week, was at that by the receiver for Chandler M. Wood January 31, at th Postponement was of the Manufacture New York, trustee, the recent death of Quatters, the fo there had been d rangements of the committee for bidd er bidders appear

Present at the Monday morning Craig of the law f Fennemore & Nai resenting the Man Co. of New York ceiver, and C. B. staff, attorney for

The original leg sale stipulated th erty of the corp its sawmills at M and Standard, an way from Holbr would be sold b public sale to the bidder. The bon 055,000 and the the Apache R amounting to $5 and other stock chinery, land, ment. The co McQuatters ap

JD made waves at the first meeting of the new Board of Supervisors in January 1935. Major Wright's employment would continue for at least one more month. *Courtesy of* the Daily Sun*; photographed by Flagstaff Public Library staff.*

position and also produced a petition signed by thirty citizens expressing the same view. After much discussion it was agreed that Major Wright keep his job another month while his past record was reviewed by a panel of nine.[35]

With that front-page rumble, JD Walkup began his prolific immersion into Flagstaff politics. He remained a member of the Chamber of Commerce, helping link the business community to the county. He was an avid supporter of jobs, tourism and improved highways. JD was a great numbers man, reeling off monetary benefits of various contracts as he kept a close eye on the county budget. His activities and opinions garnered attention from the *Sun* in almost every issue. To be fair, civic matters were on the minds of many of the town's people in this post-Depression period. All the city council and county board meetings were covered by the paper and none of the elected officials avoided scrutiny. However, it appeared to be no secret that JD Walkup enjoyed the attention of holding court.

What was Marie doing all this time? We know the Walkups had three children when JD was sworn in and a fourth would soon arrive. Elizabeth, nicknamed Phoebe by her doting siblings, would be Marie's last child and was born on November 26, 1935. The young mother would have had her hands full, as her husband was frequently absent even when in town. The family had finally settled into the spacious two-story clapboard house at 601 North Leroux. The home was—is—situated on a corner lot and came with a covered garage and guesthouse as well as a fenced front yard. While JD's weeks were consumed with meetings, luncheons and trips to Phoenix, Marie would have had her children and the house to look after. At some point her

The Walkup home of 1937. JD had a short walk down Leroux Street to his office in the Monte Vista. The downstairs bedrooms were off a hallway behind the fireplace. *Author's collection.*

friend Alice Weston, La La, began to help with the children and doubtless provided Marie with much-needed companionship.

Throughout 1936, JD's involvement in civic matters widened and he enjoyed good press and frequent accolades from the *Sun*. The paper itself had expanded to cover more social events than bridge clubs and afternoon teas. Golf had become a favorite local sport with women's and men's leagues competing at the Flagstaff Country Club. The packed-dirt course north of town by now had its spacious yet rustic clubhouse on site. Luncheons and parties as well as evening dances hosted by club members became the norm. Tennis was another sport that gained in popularity that decade and local tournaments were followed closely. Church-sponsored clothing drives and fund-raisers were still given print space but events from new clubs and the schools were too. The Local Brevities page had been renamed Personals and kept the locals informed on how their neighbors were faring in the rapidly expanding town. Little Tommy was recovering from a broken shoulder, Suzie Smith had a bad case of pneumonia and JD Walkup said the water situation looked good for the summer. These two- or three-sentence entries wove a story and reminded the reader it was still a community. Interestingly, however, nowhere in the *Sun*'s chatty pages was there a mention of Marie Walkup.

Summer gave way to autumn, and plans were afoot for next year's All-Indian Powwow. Winter still had to be reckoned with, however, and it was shaping up to be a snowy one. January 1937 saw five to six feet of the heavy wet stuff and it was reported that a white dusting even covered the deserts of Phoenix that year. Flagstaff came to a standstill for more than a week and the repercussions from the storms lasted into March. Flooding was a major problem, as were caved-in roofs and dead livestock. It was springtime before the town shook itself loose and emerged from their homes once again.[36]

Baseball and softball teams began to organize in April that year and Flagstaff was in the running to host the Western Baseball Tournament that summer. Although it was ultimately played in Phoenix, it was an exciting prospect and was an indication of how favorably the town was now viewed. Multiple organizations, ranging from the 20–30 Club to Arizona's Wool Growers, made plans to hold their 1937 regional conventions in Flagstaff. As the weather warmed from May into June, the town returned to its usual vibrancy. Skimming through pages of the *Sun* one sees familiar names from the 1920s. Tim and Caroline Riordan now spent much of their time visiting daughter Mary Chambers's family after losing their beloved daughter Ann to polio in late '27. The Babbitt family remained a vital presence in town but

THE COCONINO SUN

School . . .

ıtinued from Page One)
; the cost under the Walters
ıbout $66,000.
special election authorized
$53,000 federal four per
nds. The government's gift
er cent of the contract cost
hus make available a little
ıan $70,000, the amount of
bid for the school complete
ssembly hall.
ı the proposition first came
school board planned a
building. But in a meet-
h representative taxpayers
decided that the total con-
rice should not exceed $50,-
more than five per cent, or
of $52,250. Arrangements
loan-gift had already been
y the trustees with federal
officials, and the contract
ı the government and the
and preliminary federal
ılities had been completed.
a new application for the
mount would have involved
60 days and would have
ed possibility of getting the
loan and 3? per cent gift.
e bond election was called,
ement on behalf of the
being made through The
t, though the ballots called
of $53,000 in bonds, only
would be sold.
lection carried.
ıssembly hall is an import-
d, to conduct a well-round-
educational program, which
directed recreations, and
use in the anticipated fed-
nericanization program. It
nned also to use its stage
ual training, and, when the
velops, for the conduct of
litional classes.
need for the new school is
iate. Steady annual in-
in our school population,
transfer of the college
g school elementary pupils
city school system, and
ınticipated mergers, make
rative that the new school
pleted this summer ready
fall term.
elimination of the assem-
ı from the plans would re-
al cost of the structure by
five and six thousand dol-

Walkup Spoke To 20-30 Group

James Walkup, as guest speaker Wednesday at the first luncheon meeting of the 20-30 club, gave an interesting account of explorations and discoveries made recently by members of the Museum of Northern Arizona staff and men connected with the national monuments of the southwest down in some of the many strange fissures in this section.

One of the fissures most extensively explored is the one known as the Ben Doney "Skeleton" mine, which Doney located as a mining claim back in the nineties and named it because of the human skeleton he found. In 1933 preliminary explorations were made by Ferrell Colton and bones of prehistoric camels were discovered, as well as other bones.

Last year and again this spring further explorations were made by Dr. Harold S. Colton, John C. McGregor, Mr. Walkup and 'Gene Gordon, engineer for the national monuments of the southwest. In the last attempt to find the bottom of the "Skeleton" mine fissure, Gordon went down about 290 feet and still found no bottom. Great danger from falling rocks was encountered.

From bones and other findings, Mr. Walkup believes the fissure was used by prehistoric people as a sacrificial graveyard and interesting discoveries may be made later. Further explorations are planned within a few weeks, he said.

The 20-30 meeting was presided over by President Alvin Lloyd. Henry Bosley was in charge of the program. One of the features of the luncheon was a birthday cake for H. C. McQuatters. Those at the meeting were Fred Moore, sponsor, Weldon Brinton, Wendell Heywood, Alvin Lloyd, Dale Cress, Alex Thompson, Wilbur Caffey, Millard Kuhn, Eddie Metz, Dwight Patterson, Karl Mangum, H. C. McQuatters, Henry Bosley, James Walkup and Melvin Hutchinson.

Calling Warrants

N. Ariz. Indian . .

(Continued from Page One)

The sum given to the Grand Canyon represents an increase of $11,000 over the annual appropriation made for the park last year. Part of the increase will be used to base a ranger at a collection and checking station on the newly improved Desert View-Cameron road.

The Grand Canyon appropriation also makes provision for extra equipment at the park hospital, and for the purchase of Indian crafts and arts to serve as exhibits at camp fire talks.

An increase was also made in the appropriations set aside each year for the southwestern group of national monuments. Included in the group are the Petrified Forest, Wupatki ruins, Sunset Crater and Walnut Canyon ruins. Jurisdiction of the funds for the monuments will be under direction of Frank Pinkley at Casa Grande.

Hearings on the interior appropriation bill were held before a senate sub-committee headed by Senator Hayden. He was also chairman of the senate conferees on the bill, and made the report which led to the bill's final adoption.

Dr. Slipher . . .

(Continued from Page One)

much at first. Only prolonged observation will yield a working knowledge of the planet.

"Earth would appear larger and brighter than Mars and bluer even than Venus. Its polar caps could be made out much less easily than those of Mars.

"Seasonal changes would in time become recognizable in other features than polar caps. The oceans and wooded areas would be nearly black, as seen through holes in the clouded atmosphere, but veiled with blue.

"Oceans of the earth and green vegetation might not always be easily differentiated. Under best observations the Nile Valley would show seasonal changes not very different from a strong canal on Mars.

College B. Now

The Arizona S
lege marching ar
der the directior
derson left Mo
the annual tour
nearly every lo
Arizona.
The band wa
and presented si
parades. Forty
trip. Student d
liams cut his fi
major.

Avail yoursel
printing service
at The Coconin

ties that some t
been turned ov
fornia bank. S
was eventually
committee to m
to the deposit
larger than the
have been.
Chandler M.
and Dr. Herma
superintendent
tion, are the ot
college board.

If you
with
Moth

TI

F

JD Walkup was well on his way to becoming one of Flagstaff's movers and shakers. By 1935, he was an elected official, a member of the Chamber of Commerce and a respected speaker at many events. *Courtesy of the* Daily Sun*; photographed by Flagstaff Public Library staff.*

The Hotel Monte Vista in 2020. While not quite the power center it was in the 1930s, the Monte V is still a popular gathering place for locals and out-of-towners. *Author's collection.*

had suffered tragedies of their own. The Pollards, Dolans and other frontier families were in the second or third generation now. New names mingled with the old-timers on the Personals page, and it appeared everyone was excited to enjoy the good weather.[37]

A seemingly trivial item that appeared in the May 7, 1937 *Sun* would be of interest in a few more years. On the Society, Church and Club News page, a banner appeared: "E.K. Martin and Miss Frances Cole Announce Marriage." The happy blurb read in part, "Announcement of the marriage of Miss Frances Cole and E.K. 'Abe' Martin was made here yesterday. The ceremony was Sunday morning, April 18, at Kingman….Miss Cole came here early in February with her brothers, Kenneth and Floyd, from Pittsburgh, Pa., for the benefit of Floyd's health….Mr. Moore is the head pharmacist at the Moore Drug store, where he has been employed since 1928….Though she has been here a comparatively short time, his bride, a charming young woman, also has made many friends here."

The All-Indian Powwow was foremost in many people's minds that summer, and it was taking up most of JD's attention. Over time the three-day event had grown in popularity and size, and this year it was going international. The eighth annual Powwow would have an hour of Native song, dance and instrumental music broadcasted live over NBC. The event

THE ALL-INDIAN POWWOW

The history of the Powwow is rooted in a decades-long attempt by the federal government to ban Native Americans from ceremonial dancing. There were some who believed these rituals prevented the tribes from assimilating into the white man's culture and others who found the dancing immoral. The ban would never take. Not only did the Native Americans consider many of their dances sacred, but there were millions of tourists over the years who came to watch the graceful, haunting and powerful rituals. The different tribes came to realize that by tying their ceremonials to one of the white man's holidays, it ensured its safety for years to come.

Flagstaff's first All-Indian Powwow was a modest affair held in 1929 over the Fourth of July and involved dancing, games and racing. The town fathers were quick to realize the potential for tourism, so they began a coordinated campaign with tribal leaders and business owners to promote the Powwow as an annual event. It was a great success and grew to include rodeos, beauty pageants, displays of pottery and jewelry and, as always, dancing.

The people attending were as varied as the dances, with Navajo, Hopi, Apache and Havasupai among the tribes represented. In the early years of the Powwow that meant traveling from great distances, and the arrival of the various tribes was an event unto itself. The Navajo arrived by wagon, some traversing hundreds of miles to participate. The Apache would ride in on horseback and often drove their livestock into town with them. The Havasupai, who still live deep in the Grand Canyon, also rode their horses and made camp in the Coconino forests.

Perusing a pamphlet from the 1939 Powwow, one can read brief descriptions of some of the more spectacular dances. The Navajo Sun Dance was akin to a war dance, with warriors costumed in eagle and hawk feathers and carrying spears. The Santa Ana Water Drum Dance was originally a healing ritual, and the Navajo Mounted Chanters' Melodies were led by a Navajo on a white horse. The Hopi Hoop Dance was part of a spiritual ritual in honor of agility and strength. Young dancers wielding a willow hoop gracefully jumped and turned as they passed it through their limbs in time to a rhythmic drumbeat. Other dances performed at Powwow included the Feather Dance, the Corn Grinding Dance, the Fire Dance and the Butterfly Dance.

Powwow evolved to include much more than pageantry and dancing. Rodeo became integral to the event, and one might be surprised to learn there are "Indian cowboys." These Native Americans could and did compete in all of the events, from bronco riding to wild horse racing. Interspersed between the contests could be a demonstration on roping a calf or milking a wild cow. There were also women's horse races as well as beauty contests and games of tug-o-war.

The last official Powwow in Flagstaff was in July 1980. Those lucky enough to have lived in the Northlands and experienced the extravaganza first-hand speak of the dancing, drumming and whirl of activities with a wistful reverence. They are memories from a different time and sensibility, never to be repeated.*

* J. Howard Pyle, "Round the World," Souvenir Program Southwest All-Indian Pow Wow, July 2, 3, 4, 1939, 12. The online exhibit had over ten souvenir programs from the 1930s to 1990, and I read through several. However, it was the July 1939 program that I took most of my information from.

would air on two continents and be voiced in French, German and English. The impact of being the first Powwow ever to broadcast live cannot be overstated. The city would be overrun with tourists from all over the United States who wanted to be present for this momentous event. Residents were encouraged to list any available rooms that they had with the city that could be rented to out-of-towners. This gave the locals extra pocket money and ensured fewer visitors would be turned away. It was a summer practice that survived for decades afterward as more organizations turned to Flagstaff as a summer host.[38]

The Powwow was a resounding success, but JD had no time to rest on his laurels. As chairman of the Board of Supervisors that year, he was frequently in Phoenix for state meetings. There was one planned for July 22 that he had to attend. His attention was also consumed by the chamber's position on state taxes, and JD was expected to make a presentation before a commission in the coming weeks. Flagstaff had just snagged the Elks' annual state jamboree event and would host that at the end of July. From all accounts, JD Walkup was a very busy man that summer and a happy one as well.

8

JULY 22, 1937

The week of July 18 was warm and dry for Flagstaff, with highs around ninety-two degrees Fahrenheit and lows at night in the upper forties. Baseball and softball dominated the pages of the *Sun* as state tournaments loomed in the weeks ahead. *Kid Galahad*, starring Edward G. Robinson and Bette Davis, was playing at the Orpheum, as well as *Ladies in Love* and *Easy Living* with Jean Arthur. A few weeks earlier, Walkup had relocated his chamber office to a space in the Monte Vista. The Monte V had become the unofficial hub for all gatherings of any import, and it was bustling with activity and excitement that summer. The hotel was also a short, pleasant walk to and from JD's home on North Leroux, which would have been convenient given his many meetings.[39]

A blurb appeared in the paper on July 16 regarding the Flagstaff girls' softball team. Managed and coached by Bill Gutherie that year, the team would be travelling to Phoenix on the twenty-second to compete in the Western State Tournament for Girls. They'd been on a roll, beating Winslow 45 to 0 at home and 21 to 2 away. A loyal and boisterous crowd attended the games, and the *Sun* covered the players with the same zest they gave the men. One of the young women on the team, Doris Gee, would end up playing an important part in JD's life decades later.

As it happened, Walkup either offered or was recruited to take several of the girls with him when he drove to Phoenix that Thursday, July 22. There were a limited number of southbound routes to the capital in 1937, each taking six to seven hours to drive, so carpooling was a practicality that people accepted. JD probably chose the most direct route that summer's day, driving several miles south of town to pick up Schnebly Hill Road. Incredibly, this narrow, winding, dirt-packed road is still in use today for vehicles possessing four-wheel drive. While deeply rutted and primitive in the extreme, it closely follows Oak Creek Canyon, a breathtaking cut through the red rocks of Sedona. JD's route would have then turned west through the town of Sedona itself before zigzagging southwest into the Cottonwood/Clarkdale area. Continuing southwest on what is now SR 89A, he'd have climbed the switchbacks of Cleopatra Hill, driven past the mining town of Jerome (elevation 5,066 feet) and then descended in a series of hairpin turns into the town of Prescott. The route continued across the primitive and beautiful high desert plateau before entering into the Prescott National Forrest. Winding through the heavily treed area, the road once again began a series of climbs and descents until, finally, it reached the desert floor at Congress, Arizona. There was still a two-hour drive into Phoenix from Congress, but the mountains and curves were behind them. Two alternate routes were available but they were slightly longer, and it's doubtful JD would have chosen them. In any case, all roads to Phoenix from the north in 1937 eventually went through Prescott.[40]

The warning signs at the north end of Schnebly Hill Road are not exaggerating. The road is deeply rutted and narrows to less than a one-way in areas. But if you can make it to Oak Creek Canyon, the scenery is spectacular! *Author's collection.*

What happened that morning in the Leroux home after JD kissed his family goodbye is murkier. There were reports that the Walkup children were seen playing outside in the yard well into the late afternoon. An article that appeared in the next morning's *Sun* said that Marie Walkup had called Dr. Fronske the day before complaining of a stomach ailment and she worried that the children may have contracted it. Fronske told reporters this was a chronic condition, and he seemed to imply that the mother of four was overreacting. However he said he did his best to reassure her over the phone and then hung up and attended to the needs of his other patients. The next evening, Thursday, he and his wife drove south to Oak Creek, where Fronske was the guest of honor at a picnic.

Sunset that Thursday was at 7:38 p.m., and the soft summer light lingered another hour or so before the full moon cast its radiance on the town. It was close to 10:30 p.m. when the telephone rang once again at Dr. Fronske's residence. His oldest son, Robert, had been entrusted to answer calls and take down any messages for his father that evening. At the other end of the line was Marie Walkup, who wanted to leave a message for the doctor. As reported on the front page of the *Sun* the following day, Robert went to get a pencil to write it down: "Please have Dr. Fronske call at the house on his early round of visits." Then after a moment she said, "Wait a minute—Be sure to tell him not tonight, but tomorrow morning."

The *Sun* reported that Robert carefully wrote down the message. When the elder Fronskes returned home shortly after midnight, Robert was awake and felt compelled to relay the information to his father before retiring. After that the *Sun*'s article is somewhat confusing, as it jumps ahead to a second note addressed to Fronske, albeit one found tacked to the Walkups' front door. Any dissembling or print error on the newspaper's part is understandable. Billie Yost, a former reporter, said in a 1978 interview, "And it happened—the *Coconino Sun* as a weekly would go to press Thursday night so that we'd have the paper ready for Friday morning. So we had to destroy the front page of the paper and we had to do it all over."[41]

Three miles north of town, the Flagstaff Country Club sat in darkness, illuminated only by the moon and a sky packed with stars. The open space provided by the golf course, bound to the east by a thick ponderosa pine forest that stretched for miles, made it an enticing place for an illicit walk, especially during the full moon. Ed Conrad was a twenty-nine-year-old sawmill worker who had surreptitiously walked the private property many times before. On this particular night he brought along three others: his date, Mariam Moore, twenty-two; his younger sister, Rose, sixteen; and Rose's

A side view of the Walkup house. The small window downstairs would be the kitchen while the upstairs window looks into Rose and John's bedroom. *Author's collection.*

date, Mark Yates. As the young people trespassed through the wooded area of the course, they laughed and enjoyed a few nips of whiskey from Ed's flask. As they rounded a point near the first hole, Ed suddenly stopped and raised his arm in silent warning to his friends. In the light of the full moon the four saw a car parked halfway off the frontage road that separated the golf course from Dr. Colton's ranch. In his previous jaunts, Ed had never seen anyone else on the course. The night was deathly silent save for the crickets chirping in the nearby brush.

Slowly the four approached the car. They could see the driver's side door was open, but still there was no sound. It was Rose who first spotted a bare foot, and she gasped audibly. Ed walked quickly toward the back of the car and peered around to the driver-side door. There in the moonlight he was greeted by a grisly sight. Lying on her back, her flimsy nightgown and robe soaked in blood, was the dead body of a woman. An old German army rifle was propped beside her, the muzzle now pointing away. One shot had been fired tearing a hole through the woman's chest, leaving blood and chunks of flesh splayed about. The slipper from her right food was off and lying nearby, as if it had been removed on purpose. The time was 12:25 a.m.[42]

Flagstaff artist Karen Raskin-Young painted this image of the Walkup car at the golf course that July night. No crime scene photos were taken of either site, so the artist relied on newspaper accounts. There's a discrepancy about whether the car was parked by the first hole or the fourth *Painter: Karen Raskin-Young; author's collection.*

Shocked and upset, the four young people hurried to their car and drove back to town to notify the authorities. Conrad dropped off his companions first before driving to the sheriff's office, where Deputy Sheriffs Perry Francis and Forrest Willis were on duty. Together the three men drove the four miles back toward the bloody scene at the country club, traveling north on a deserted Fort Valley Road before turning east onto Schultz Pass Road. As they continued on the isolated, winding drive to the clubhouse, they spotted the vehicle standing in silhouette by the moonlight. As they parked their own vehicle and approached on foot, Deputy Francis was struck with a realization—he recognized the car as belonging to JD Walkup. Several thoughts went through his mind as he tried to make sense of this. In a town of five thousand, the sheriff's office knew most of the people and a great deal about their private business. A prominent citizen like Walkup was even more visible, and his comings and goings were well-publicized in the *Sun*. Francis knew that JD had left for Phoenix Thursday morning—in fact, he'd reportedly given a lift to a few of the softball players.

As Ed Conrad pointed to where the trespassers had found the body, Francis and Willis approached the car. The body of the young woman lay where it had been discovered less than an hour before. Her face, while twisted into a rictus, was not affected by the gaping wound to her chest. There was no question but that Marie Walkup was dead. As his training kicked in, Deputy Francis took charge of the scene. A coroner's jury must be brought to the site, so he ordered Conrad and Willis to stay with the body. As he drove back into town, Francis stopped to rouse Dr. Schermann, the county health officer, and notified coroner Max Miller. He called for reinforcements to the sheriff's office and then the three men formulated a plan. They would be returning to the scene for the official jury but first there was a stop they needed to make. If JD Walkup was indeed in Phoenix and Marie was lying dead outside her car, someone needed to check on the Walkup children.

The three officials made the short drive up the sloping Leroux and parked in front of the Walkup house. All was quiet as they walked through the front gate and climbed the three steps onto the porch. A piece of paper nailed to the front door caught one of the men's eyes. Addressed to Dr. Fronske the note said simply, "Look inside the bedrooms." Off to one side of the door was an empty milk bottle that contained another piece of furled paper. Opening it, the men read the cryptic message: "No milk today." One of the officials went to notify Dr. Fronske; however, which one and by what means is not documented. The remaining two men tried the door and, finding it unlocked, decided to enter the home. They would confine themselves to the downstairs, but given what they discovered, the decision was an intelligent one.

As they stepped inside the front door they found themselves in a house that looked quite familiar to 1930s Flagstaff. To their left was a small breakfast nook that opened into a kitchen. A quick glance showed nothing out of order in either room. Proceeding to their right, the men made their way through the spacious living room with its fireplace on the north wall. A short hallway was just beyond this area, at the back of the house. A door to the right opened into a child's bedroom; down the hall to the left was the parents' room. They opened the door on the right and looked inside.

The small bedroom held both a crib and a child-sized bed. Moving closer to the crib the men saw baby Elizabeth, a few days shy of twenty months old. She was lying quite still on her back, a teddy bear tucked under her chin. The toddler made no sounds as she lay there, nor did she move about in her tiny cocoon. Just a few steps away, in a small, neat bed, lay ten-year-old Daniel. As the men bent down to examine him more closely they detected no sound of breath entering and leaving the boy's body.

A very good rendition of the actual stairs inside the Walkup home, leading to Rose and John's bedroom. *Painter: Karen Raskin-Young; author's collection.*

MOTHER, FOUR CHILDREN FOUND DEAD LAST NIGHT

Ball Tourney Opens Sunday

FOURTEEN TEAMS ENTER WESTERN STATES EIGHT-DAY ELIMINATION PLAY

California, Utah, New Mexico And Arizona Compete—Arbelbide Adds Prescott Stars To Local Team

A Republican Prays

SCARED HORSE CAUSES DEATH OF ELI LUCERO

IS BUILDING FINE NEW RESIDENCES

Frank Sufea Plans Homes For Six Families

BROADCAST WAS CLEAR IN SWEDEN

Several Kachina Dances Scheduled

BODY OF MRS. JAMES D. WALKUP NEAR COUNTRY CLUB, OTHERS IN THEIR BEDS AT FAMILY HOME

First Inkling Of The Terrible Tragedy Discovered After Midnight By Moonlight Hiking Party

MR. WALKUP WAS IN PHOENIX

Children Stabbed With Fine Instrument—Mother Left Notes For Husband, Doctor And Milkman

Elks Jamboree Begins Wednesday

KIWANIS CLUB CHARTER NIGHT IS AUGUST 12

Richardson Makes Big Improvements At Cameron Post

Lumber Carriers For Local Mills

FIVE NIGHTS OF RIOTOUS FUN UNDER BIG TENTS ELKS LODGE SPONSORING

Show Grounds At Aspen And Agassiz—Will Be 17 Different Attractions—Elks Have Concessions

Circus Lost?

Band Tonight

The July 23, 1937 edition of the *Coconino Sun* had already been put to bed when the murders-suicide was discovered. Staff came in and rewrote the front page. *Courtesy the* Daily Sun; *photographed by Flagstaff Public Library staff.*

There was no sign of blood or violence in the room or on the bodies. Both children were dressed in clean pajamas and tucked into beds that were clearly made with fresh sheets. It was only when the men pulled back the covers that they noticed the ugly bruises around the throats of both of the children. The officials quickly retreated from the house and returned to the porch to await Dr. Fronske.

At approximately 1:30 a.m., the doctor arrived and, after a terse conversation, entered the home with at least one of the trio. Fronske was familiar with the Walkup house, and within a few minutes he headed up the narrow stairs to another bedroom. He never spoke publicly about what he was feeling that night, but one can easily imagine the dread that filled his heart over what he might find. As he entered the children's room, he would not have been unprepared.

The upstairs bedroom was much like the one on the ground floor except that two small beds were contained inside. There was no movement from either of the tiny figures lying on them, each child covered with a fresh sheet that was pulled up to their chin. Rose Marie, almost eight, and John, four and a half, appeared to be asleep from a distance. The room was deathly quiet, and no sign of blood was evident. Dr. Fronske moved closer to inspect the bodies and, pulling back the covers, saw the same ugly bruising on their necks as was on Elizabeth's and Danny's. At least one more note, addressed to JD, was found on the scene and reprinted in the papers the following day.

The four small bodies were taken to the county morgue, only a few blocks from the home. There they were laid out on a cold table and given a visual exam. It's quite possible this is where the full extent of their injuries was discovered. Quoting from the July 23, 1937 *Sun*: "After four o'clock this morning, at Flagstaff Undertaking parlors, it was discovered that the three younger children were stabbed directly over the heart area with a fine instrument....A strange circumstance, that delayed the finding of the stab wounds, was that there was no blood on the beds, the nightclothes, or the children's bodies....There was a man's handkerchief knotted at two corners and twisted that is believed may have been used as a tourniquet."

The *Sun* was almost certainly wrong in that it wasn't the three younger children who had identical injuries. The discrepancy lay in the extent of Rose's injuries and what actually happened to her that night. All four death certificates are identical regarding the principal cause and manner of death. Each certificate states that the child was "stabbed in the chest in the heart area" and then strangled. However, Max Miller, who as justice of the peace assembled the coroner's jury, was quoted in the paper as saying Rose had been stabbed only once and that the weapon did not penetrate deeply. Rather, he believed it hit the young girl's rib and was deflected off of it. The other three children, Miller said, were stabbed twice directly over the heart.

The *Sun* also reported these observations in its hurried article for the July 23 paper: "There were bruise marks on the throats of three, and on the throat of one a slight laceration, as though from a fingernail....The elder girl had been stabbed only once, and the instrument, it was thought, did not penetrate deeply but was deflected by a rib....The coroner's jury verdict at 4:30 this morning was that the children died from stab wounds and strangulation inflicted by the mother, who they decided, had committed suicide shortly before midnight."

Miller might have speculated more freely when talking with the *Arizona Republic*, or perhaps the *Coconino Sun* was reluctant to print the prurient details. In any case, the accounts between the two papers differed in that the Phoenix paper went into greater detail. Miller told the *Republic* that Marie Walkup "had committed the murders with such dispatch that nothing was

Page Six THE COCON

MOTHER, FOUR CHILDREN FOUND DEAD LAST NIGHT

(Continued from Page One)

There was another note addressed to "Mama and Arrietta," recommending how various household articles should be disposed of.

Mrs. Walkup, who was about 35 years of age, attractive and home-loving, had many friends here made both before and since her marriage. For some time she lived with Mr. and Mrs. T. E. Pollock of this city. She also had clerked in the Babbitt store. Her maiden name was Green.

Justice of Peace Max W. Miller called the following coroner's jury: Phil Hollingsworth, Paul Shinpnick, W. B. McKeeth, Frank Shawhart, H. E. Mason and Dolph Bassett.

The little children were all dead when the house was entered. The baby, Phoebe, about two years old, was in her little crib bed in a down stairs bedroom; Dannie, the oldest child, about 10, in a bed in the same room, and Rose Marie, about eight, and Jackie, five, in a room in two beds upstairs. There was a cloth around the baby's head. They were all dressed for bed.

There were bruise marks on the throats of three, and on the throat of one a slight laceration, as though from a fingernail.

After four o'clock this morning, at Flagstaff Undertaking parlors, it was discovered that the three younger children each had been stabbed directly over the heart area with a fine instrument. The elder girl had been stabbed only once, and the instrument, it was thought, did not penetrate deeply but was deflected by a rib.

A strange circumstance, that delayed finding of the stab wounds, was that there was no blood on the beds, the nightclothes, or the children's bodies. But a wash cloth was found with a small spot of blood on it. There

Ferrell Colton Completes Book, "Last Of The Square-Rigged Ships," And Will Take It To Publisher In New York City

Ferrell Colton will leave the last of this week or first of next for New York city with manuscript for a book he is just completing—"Last of the square-rigged ships," to be published by G. P. Putnam and Sons.

The author since early boyhood at the Atlantic coast has made a hobby of sailing, has made many friends among masters of vessels, and last year completed a voyage before the mast around the world on a cargo-carrying sailship.

The book is entirely factual and lists all existing square-rigged ships in or out of service that still carry their yards. There are 313 of them of which all but 13 are in actual service.

Names of as many as possible were secured from the Lloyds lists, but there are many Lloyds did not have listed. Mr. Colton sent forms to every builder, owner and shipmaster. From their replies he has compiled a description of each vessel with measurements, its history, complete roster of its passages and time in days of each passage.

From this data the initiated reader can judge pretty accurately for himself the vessel's capacity, sail area and speed.

The book will contain about 300 pages. There are 75 prints of boats, all from photos, many taken by the author himself, others obtained through a London friend prominently identified with ocean shipping and others through a London agency and from contributors the world over.

Guam Official A Visitor Here

Hon. Baltasor J. Bordello, chairman of the House of Council Congress of Guam, was here Wednesday enroute from Washington, D. C., to Pasadena. He visited Raymond Prochnow. They were classmates at St. Mary's college a number of years ago.

Mr. Bordello was traveling across the country in a car accompanied by his chauffeur and planned to stop at Pasadena to visit another classmate, Jack Sutherland, an attorney.

He had been to Washington, where he had a personal conference with the president and congressional leaders regarding right of citizens of Guam to vote. He said the president promised to visit the island this fall. Mr. Bordello had been in the states since the first of the year, when congress first convened. This mission that he had been on for his people is the highest honor that could be bestowed upon a resident of the island, he said. From Pasadena he planned to sail for Honolulu and from there take the China Clipper to Guam. Guam, one of the refueling stops for the Clipper.

Guam, or Guahan is one of the Ladrone group of islands in the Pacific and one of the most important naval and refueling bases,

Page six of the July 23, 1937 *Coconino Sun*. Surprisingly few mistakes were made in reporting the tragedy, given that the paper's staff had to rewrite the front page in the early morning hours. *Courtesy the* Daily Sun*; photographed by Flagstaff Public Library staff.*

out of place—the children, night clothes and bedding were in order." The article also painted a horrific scenario of the evening's events, relying heavily on Miller's deductions:

> *Sometime during the early morning hours, the mother, Mrs. Walkup, slipped quietly into the bedrooms of her children. When she emerged a short time later, with an army rifle under her arm, Coroner Max Miller reported, the children…were silent in death. Then Mrs. Walkup entered the family car and sped to the nearby Flagstaff gold* [sic] *course. Holding the rifle to her body, Miller deduced, she discharged the rifle with one of her feet. Four hitchhikers found her torn body, attired only in a flimsy nightgown and dressing robe, about daylight.…With the exception of Rose Marie, whose body indicated she had awakened and resisted her mother, the children all died without struggling…Their mother made certain her death dealing was effective, Miller reported. He said she strangled the children after stabbing them. Elizabeth, the baby, had a tiny toy teddy bear propped under her chin to keep the mouth from dropping open.*[43]

Several of the statements in the *Republic* are assuredly wrong, such as the timing of the killings and the suicide. Ed Conrad found Marie at 12:25 a.m. and the children are assumed to have died around 10:00 p.m. Regardless of the errant details, news of the maternal filicide that had occurred in Flagstaff spread quickly throughout the state and western region. Within a few days, the Walkup family murders and suicide had been reported in most major newspapers in the United States and several overseas.[44]

JD, asleep in his Phoenix hotel room and unaware that life as he knew it had been destroyed, was awakened by a persistent knocking on the door. It was the night clerk, telling the gentleman from Flagstaff that he had to return home immediately. The clerk was evidently vague about the why because JD called Deputy Sheriff Charlie Marshall and asked him what had happened. Marshall finally told JD that Marie was dead but said nothing about the children. The hapless man left for Flagstaff at once, retracing the route he had traveled less than twenty-four hours earlier. An article in the July 30, 1937 *Coconino Sun* gave this detailed account:

> *Mr. Walkup, advised at Phoenix from the sheriff's office here as soon as possible after the tragedy was discovered that Mrs. Walkup was dead, left at once by automobile alone and reached here early Friday morning. Intimate friends said it was the first time he had ever returned from a trip from any distance without bringing presents for each of his children. He drove at once to the sheriff's office, where he learned that his wife had taken her own life. He asked where the children were, and then the full extent of his loss was revealed to him as gently as possible.*

Marie had left several notes at the house beside the two found outside on the porch. One of the notes was addressed to her husband, and the *Sun* printed at least a portion of it on the July 23 front page: "Because of my lack of discipline—the children are happier to go this way. Only grief would come to them. You are strong in faith, never doubting—mercy to my people. I love you and I have failed. Let La La help you and the service be private. She will find what things we need."

The last of the four notes found at the scene was addressed to "Mama and Arrieta" and was said to have detailed how the service was to be conducted as well as disposal of several household items.

Friends and family of JD were with him constantly in the days that followed. Marie's relatives came to Flagstaff from California and Colorado to attend the private ceremony held on Monday, July 26. The *Sun* reported

SPARKS from the GRIND-STONE by COLUMBUS GIRAGI

The Coconino Sun

ARIZONA'S GREATEST WEEKLY NEWSPAPER

Volume 55 | Single Copy—5 Cents | Flagstaff, Arizona, July 30, 1937 | By the Year—$2.50

THOUSANDS MAKE MERRY AT FLAGSTAFF ELKS BIG CARNIVAL AND JAMBOREE

Began Wednesday For Five Nights Of Fun And Frolic Under The Big Tents —17 Different Attractions

Osborn Is Named Legion Convention Committee Head

RITES TRAGEDY VICTIMS HELD HERE MONDAY

Mrs. Walkup, Four Children Are Laid In Masonic Cemetery

Last Rites Mrs. Agnes Pouthie Wednesday

BASEBALL AT ITS HO[ME] FLAGSTAF[F]

Purse Snatcher Held Under Bond

STATE GOLF TOURNEY IS NEXT WEEK

Annual Invitational Is Bringing Many Visitors

National Guard Adopts Schedule

Kiwanians Have A Social Hour

Swinnerton Is A Visitor Here

Charles Young Cattleman Dies At Grand Canyon

To Sound-Color Film State Nat'l Guard Work Here

Car Hit Truck; New Yorker Hurt

Expects Reservati[on] Road Improvem[ent]

LEGIONAIR[E] AUTO RAC[E] AUGUST [2]

Day After Close Legion's State Convention

The *Coconino Sun* was a weekly paper. The July 30 edition reported on the burial as well as the impact the tragedy had on JD and the community. *Courtesy the* Daily Sun; *photographed by Flagstaff Public Library staff.*

"many beautiful floral offerings" crowding the Flagstaff Undertaking parlors as Reverend Joseph Doran, Episcopalian minister, conducted the morning service. The sad parade of vehicles carrying one large casket and four smaller was followed by cars bearing the few invited family members. The caravan made its way south over the tracks to Citizens Cemetery where, upon entering, they made an immediate right to continue the short drive to the Masonic section of the grounds. It was there in one large plot that the four Walkup children were buried side by side. In the same raised square, Marie was buried at the head of and at a right angle to the caskets of her children. At some point a large tree grew in the center of the Walkup plot, separating the mother from her offspring. It has since been cut down, leaving only a stump as a reminder.

Most of JD's relatives traveled from Tennessee to attend the funerals and offer him support. His sister, Mrs. R.B. Dixon of Nashville, and her daughter Betty, stayed in Flagstaff to help him further. The *Sun* reported they rented an apartment and planned to "keep house" for the shaken man until he could manage for himself. As far as the civic duties that crowded his calendar, the *Sun* reported this:

> *Mr. Walkup said yesterday that he will probably leave for about 10 days after the monthly meeting, next Monday, of the county supervisors. He wishes to rest and be free of all responsibilities for a while. He has turned over his work at the chamber of commerce, of which he is secretary, to his assistant there, Mrs. Jeff Ferris. Miss Margaret (Billie) Ennis is temporarily helping Mrs. Ferris. Mr. Walkup is chairman of the county board of supervisors and will be relieved by members Joe Tissaw and Bob Thurston…of any work there.*

The cemetery's front gate. Once inside, the sad parade of hearses made an immediate right and proceeded down the narrow road to the Masonic section of Citizens Cemetery. *Author's collection.*

The article went on to name several imminent projects JD was involved with and who would be taking over the lead. However, true to his printed word, he was back at his duties by early September, chairing meetings and pushing tourism for the city that rallied around him in his time of dreadful need.[45]

9

THE AFTERMATH

The terrible events of July 22, 1937, which left Flagstaff "a city in mourning," were never again mentioned in print for the next eight decades. The January 7, 1938 issue of the *Coconino Sun* did a month-by-month recap of the year before, detailing events trivial and important that affected the community. Under the month of July, no mention was made of Marie Walkup and her murdered children. As spring turned into summer the town's rhythms followed the predictable pattern. In the community, most people were optimistic and looking forward to the tourist season. Baseball and softball teams had formed and were being closely scrutinized as well as cheered as the season played on. The country club was open and in full swing after being closed for the winter. Meanwhile, the July 4 Powwow was given top priority and was planned with an eye toward expansion and topping last year's success.

JD Walkup continued in his role as chairman of the County Board of Supervisors and secretary of the Chamber of Commerce. His name showed up in connection with other civic interests and he expanded his reach into agriculture and aviation. Walkup appeared to have regained some of his feisty resistance to various peculiarities of government. Under the headline "Resigns from Impotent County Welfare Board," a March 4, 1938 *Sun* article read in part:

> *Following a meeting with P.H. Brooks, state commissioner of Social Security and Welfare, Saturday, JD Walkup, chairman of the county*

> *welfare board, said that he will resign at a meeting of the county board of supervisors Monday, stating he sees no reason for a county set-up when given to understand by Mr. Brooks that it has no administrative authority....It is Mr. Walkup's opinion that, if the board has no power to function except as a buffer for the state board when difficulties arise, there is no reason for it existing.*

JD was frequently mentioned in the paper that year, but it was usually in connection with his duties. An occasional blurb on the Personals page had Walkup visiting Holbrook, Winslow or another small town in the company of a male friend. He was not on the guest lists as attending any of the popular "themed" parties, such as the Mad Hatters Fete or the Chinese Dinner that year. Neither did he make an appearance at any of the galas and dances held that summer. JD occasionally served as an escort, ferrying women from Phoenix to Flagstaff whenever their schedules coincided. When his name was linked to members of Flagstaff's powerful elite—as it often was—it was only through politics and civic organizations. At least through 1938, JD kept a low social profile, and the town kept a compassionate eye on the bereaved man.[46]

Time marched on, as it always does, and brought some surprises the following year. It's impossible to glean from current sources if the town's collective tongue was wagging, but one supposes it must have been. In the August 25, 1939 *Sun*, a blurb appeared on the Personals page: "Mr. and Mrs. Sidney Sullivan, Mr. and Mrs. J.D. Walkup and Floyd Cole attended the Snake Dance at Mishongnovi Wednesday."

JD had remarried—but that alone would not have caused the stir. His new wife was the former Francis Martin, née Cole. As written in chapter seven, Francis Cole married pharmacist E.K. "Abe" Martin on April 18, 1937—less than two and a half years earlier and about two months before the July 22 tragedy.

This blurb that appeared months later in the September 1, 1939 Personals was also revealing: "Dr. and Mrs. R.L. Corbin of Luverne, Ia. will arrive Sunday for a two weeks visit with Mrs. E.K. Martin and Abe."

Apparently, Abe had moved on as well in his private life. On page three of the same issue, in the Flagstaff Social, Club and Church News, Billie Yost penned an account of a tea honoring Mrs. Jack Richardson. Listed among the Riordans, Babbitts, Knowles and Midgleys was Mrs. Abe Martin; the new Mrs. Walkup was not in attendance. This theme repeated itself in the months that followed. While the Walkups were not snubbed in the

Sun's coverage, they were usually reported in the company of one or two other couples. They were seldom on the guest list for the big parties and celebrations reported on the social pages.[47]

From late 1939 to 1941, information on Walkup is spotty. From available records it appears that sometime in 1939, JD was off the county board. The county payroll was published regularly, and Walkup's name had disappeared from the roster. Perhaps he decided he'd had enough or knew he wouldn't win his seat again. However, he remained secretary of the chamber that year and appeared to be quite active. All was not right in Walkup's private life though. According to Keith Robinson's research, JD made the decision to re-join the war effort that was building against hostilities in Europe. Although the United States did not officially enter World War II until December 7, 1941, the troops were gathering, and JD felt drawn to reenlist. What happened in Walkup's marriage to Francis Cole is not clear, but the couple divorced at some point. JD then served thirty-three months in the South Pacific and returned to Flagstaff in 1943 after being wounded in battle. This would have been the second time for Walkup; he was gassed in World War I, an incident that led him out west in 1920. His obituary noted that JD served as an army major during World War II.[48]

If Walkup did return to Flagstaff, he didn't stay for very long. No mention of him is found in the *Sun* from 1946 forward, and he had most likely relocated to Phoenix by then. It is known that JD lived the duration of his life in the greater Phoenix area, where he built a new career around his military service. In 1971, Walkup retired from the Arizona State Employment Service, where he'd worked as a veterans' employment representative. Sadly, JD didn't have much time to enjoy his retirement; he passed away the following year at age seventy-two.

However, Walkup was fortunate enough to have found love one more time. Doris Gee was a student in Flagstaff at Arizona State College when her softball team made it to the playoffs that July 22, 1937. Whether she was one of the young women JD gave a lift to that awful day is unknown; however, over a decade later, the two met again. Doris was a beautiful young woman and was employed as an educator when she and JD met. They eventually married, with the wedding taking place in Los Angeles on July 25, 1948. Several years later Doris gave birth to a son who the couple named James. James Walkup the son is still alive and living in Arizona and has children of his own.

It's been difficult to trace the history of other players in the Walkup family saga. Marie's sister, Arietta, had married Earl Allman, a Flagstaff boy, long before the tragedy. They were living in California in July 1937 and returned to Los Angeles after the funerals. No information on what became of them in the years after has been found. Searches on Marie's brother and parents likewise produced no results. The remainder of Francis Walkup Martin, née Cole's, life is also unknown, despite research into her past. No mention of her is found after 1946 in the local paper. It appears that a few of JD's siblings followed him from Tennessee to Phoenix in later years, but it's been difficult to confirm these facts. Walkup's relatives have not responded to requests to correspond.

As mentioned throughout the book, it appears the town decided to either bury the memory of that July night or discuss it only among themselves. Regardless of the scant information available on JD and the others, people who hear of the Walkup tragedy for the first time have the same reaction. Beyond the horror, they express relief that this man who suffered the horrendous loss of his children and wife went on to find happiness in his later years.

10

FILICIDE

FACTS AND FALLACIES

The National Institute of Health defines filicide as the murder of a child or children up to the age of eighteen by one or both parents. Marie Walkup committed maternal filicide when she stabbed and then strangled Daniel, Rose Marie, John and baby Elizabeth. That she then went on to commit suicide afterward is not so uncommon. While it is horrifying to even consider a parent killing their offspring, filicide has been with us forever and has been dramatized and studied for centuries. Grimm's Fairy Tales lives up to its authors' name, especially when depicting stepmothers, and what English student hasn't at least heard of Euripides's *Medea*?

In the article "An Overview of Filicide" by Sara G. West, MD, the murder of a child or children by a parent has been broken down into five categories. This system was first developed by Dr. Phillip Resnick in 1969 after studying this tragic phenomenon in several countries. The first category, and the one most associated with suicide by the offender, is the altruistic filicide. In this act the parent kills the child/children because they believe it is for their own good. They might believe their offspring cannot survive in a cold, heartless world, or perhaps the child is ill or deformed and the parent does not want them to suffer. The second category is the acutely psychotic filicide in which, as the name implies, there is no apparent rational reason for the act. The next group has been labeled the unwanted child filicide, in which the offspring is viewed as holding back the parent in some way. This includes the parent who benefits financially by the child's death, as with an insurance payout, as well as the adult who wants to start life anew and unencumbered. Some would consider Susan Smith, the mother who allowed her two little toddlers to drown in a submerged car in 1994, as fitting in here. Category four is the accidental filicide, in which a child who is subject to abuse and neglect dies as a result of the trauma, even though death is unintended. The last category to be identified is the spouse revenge filicide, with motivations similar to those depicted in the classic *Medea*. Surprisingly, this is the least likely cause of a parent killing their child/children that Resnick found in his study.[49]

It's worth noting that the 1969 study on filicide included both mothers and fathers. Later, Resnick broke down the classification of victims even further. Neonaticide refers to the murder of a newborn within the first twenty-four hours of life by a parent, and infanticide applies to a child under the age of one. In the decades that followed, Resnick and other professionals began to gather statistics, completing studies that included maternal filicide, filicide followed by suicide, the impact of depression and substance abuse on filicide and more. Before the studies were widely published, many therapists believed that having children was a mitigating factor *against* suicide. These new findings suggested otherwise and were used to educate therapists dealing with suicidal patients who were also parents.[50]

What can we find in the various studies that might shed some light on Marie Walkup's state of mind and intentions that July evening? In a 2008 paper by Friedman, et al., titled "Maternal Filicide and Its Intersection with Suicide," several interesting factors were identified. As with Resnick's 1969 findings, mothers who committed filicide and then suicide were likely to do so for altruistic reasons. Most of these women were married, and the average age was thirty-two. The majority of the women studied killed all of their minor children; however, unlike the Walkup murders, almost all used the same method of killing on both themselves and their offspring. The method used in 70 percent of cases was a firearm. The average age of the children killed was three to nine. A diagnosis of depression was found in 70 percent of the women prior to the incident, while a history of alcohol or drug abuse was rare.[51]

Another fascinating article written in 2007 by Friedman and Resnick potentially creates insight into the Walkup family tragedy. "Child Murder by Mothers: Patterns and Preventions" focused on maternal filicide and included data from incidents where the killing was followed by suicide. This paper summarized studies from fourteen countries that both presented statistics and offered strategies to prevent a potential tragedy. Some findings seem applicable to Marie Walkup's situation:

> *The mothers were often poor, socially isolated, full-time caregivers, who were victims of domestic violence or had other relationship problems. Disadvantaged socioeconomic backgrounds and primary responsibility for the children were common. Persistent crying or child factors were sometimes precipitants for the filicide. Some mothers had previously abused the child, while others were mentally ill and devoted to their children....Many of the perpetrators had psychosis, depression or suicidality....A significant proportion (16–29%) of filicides end in completed suicide by the mother... most frequently, these mothers have altruistic motives.*

While from the outside the Walkup household did not appear to be suffering financially, we can only surmise their economic situation was stable. The shadow of the Great Depression was still looming over the nation, and it's difficult to assess what impact it had on the psyche of a young mother. From the weekly postings of JD's civic activities, it's clear Marie was the primary caregiver and was likely alone much of the day. Whether Alice Weston was helping out once a day or once a week cannot be discerned at this late date. Also, despite being painted posthumously by the *Coconino Sun* as "attractive and fun-loving...had many friends here both before and since her marriage," there is little evidence that Marie was involved with or accepted by the community.[52]

The note Marie left in the Walkup house addressed to JD supports an altruistic motive for the murders of her children. Its contents suggest despair and hopelessness, which is synonymous with severe depression. Marie had also reached out several times to Dr. Fronske with vague worries about an intestinal ailment; perhaps that was her cry for help, unarticulated as it was. Fronske stated publicly that Mrs. Walkup was fearful: "Wednesday afternoon Mrs. Walkup called on Dr. Fronske. She seemed very nervous, he said. She imagined she had an intestinal ailment and worried the children might have it."[53]

One wonders why she was so concerned that the children had contracted this disorder. Was the baby fussy? Did Danny or Rose actually complain of an upset stomach? The only information we have on the little ones' health is that they were seen playing outside Thursday afternoon.

The *Arizona Republic* printed a slightly different version of Dr. Fronske's statements: "Dr. M.G. Fronske, family physician, said Mrs. Walkup had been despondent in recent weeks over a chronic intestinal ailment, and had expressed fears the children might have contracted it….She had talked to Dr. Fronske yesterday concerning the asserted ailment…she telephoned his home about 10 o'clock last night…[but] she did not require him."[54]

From the above article it appears that Marie Walkup had been under Fronske's care for a chronic problem and that her fears had escalated over the past month. Whether her concerns for the children were new or had been raised before is not documented.

The 2007 researchers readily admitted the difficulty in studying the motivations of someone who, by definition, had committed suicide and is now deceased. Many cases relied on notes left by the mother or of a past psychiatric history. They did find that those who committed filicide-suicide were less likely to be delusional than mothers who killed their children and then either survived a suicide attempt or did not attempt it at all. In all probability, this is because a delusional person would have difficulty planning the steps necessary to complete the two acts successfully.

I reached out to Dr. Elizabeth Caspian, MD, a psychiatrist with over twenty-five years of experience practicing medicine. I sent her the above articles as well as historical information specific to the Walkup situation. She was kind enough to answer general questions about filicide and toss around various possibilities with me. Most of what follows is pure speculation as there are no medical records, diaries or writings available from the concerned parties. However, I found Dr. Caspian's insights a jarring reminder that Marie Walkup was neither the cookie-cutter wife and mother nor the tragic figure painted by the *Sun*.[55]

Dr. Caspian was familiar with the studies by Resnick, Friedman, et al., on maternal filicide-suicide. As far as the statistics go, Marie seemed to fit into the averages with a few exceptions. The methods she used to kill her children were literally "hands on" as opposed to death by gunshot, which she reserved for herself. That Marie later drove twenty minutes north of town to a public place to commit suicide also struck Caspian as significant. "It takes intense, emotional energy to drive a car such a distance after killing your children. And then to create, in a sense, a public spectacle—it has the feel of vengeance and anger."

Caspian was struck by the adventurous spirit Marie showed early in her marriage. Jumping on a train and heading east toward the Cibicue trading post, albeit with JD, showed a fearlessness not many 1920s women possessed. The young couple lived on the Apache Reservation for over a year, an isolated if starkly beautiful area. Caspian expressed a thought that never had occurred to me: "When they lived out on the trading post Marie had her husband all to herself. I imagine they would have grown very close, being as isolated as they were. When they came back to Flagstaff, how did Marie feel about the move? Was she angry that she now had to share her husband with his job and the town?"

Besides the stress of becoming a mother for the first time, the couple might have experienced some economic insecurity around the time of Daniel's birth. Remember, JD quit working for Frank Brooks that spring when he went into competition with him, and Walkup's venture was ultimately a failure. The couple moved at least once in town before relocating to Coyote Range during the Depression. By that time the family had grown to four with the addition of Rose Marie. JD maintained a steady job and income while working for Dr. Colton, which was no small blessing in the early 1930s. Whatever closeness the couple had while living at the trading post might have been rekindled during the years they lived at the ranch. While not nearly as isolated as Cibicue, it was nevertheless outside of town. However, with the birth of John in 1933 followed by JD's decision to run for county supervisor, additional stress was inevitably placed on Marie with her duties as mother and wife.

Dr. Caspian noted the "spotlight" that shone on JD as he entered public life. The Depression had receded, and the family was once again living in Flagstaff proper. Did Marie have any input into her husband's latest venture into politics? What did she think of a community that followed his every movement but apparently had little interest in her? Or was it actually the other way around—did Marie shun the townspeople, most notably the women? In any case, Caspian was struck by the prominent role the newspaper—especially the Personals page—played in the life of the community:

> *It seems they functioned a bit like Facebook does today—you could follow your neighbors' comings and goings and check how popular you were if you're being covered. A lot of people get their self-esteem from what connections they have on a public platform. Which leads to another question—was JD ashamed of his wife? Was Marie "liked" enough? He was out there, she was not. It's like they're not on the same page as a couple. And if they were close at one time, she could be grieving the loss of her relationship with him. He seems to have been consumed by his work; she had the house and children.*

What were the expectations of a county supervisor's wife as JD began his new job? I find it significant that Marie Walkup didn't have a lot of time to figure out an answer to this. Within eleven months of her husband starting in his new role, baby Elizabeth was born. Once again Marie's attention would be focused on her children and home. Did this make her happy or was she depressed and upset, unable to verbalize her distress? Did she relish her role as wife and mother or could she be using it as an acceptable means to avoid social interactions? It might seem presumptuous to ask these questions but given what happened eighteen months later something was obviously very wrong.

I asked Dr. Caspian if she had any insight into Marie's calls to Dr. Fronske and the "stomach ailment" he deemed illusionary. "It wasn't that long ago that 'hysteria' was the common diagnosis for women's complaints. Their symptoms were often ignored or dismissed as a bad case of nerves. If only in retrospect, it's obvious that Marie Walkup was in a lot of emotional pain. Her immediate family was not in the area, her husband didn't notice her distress—she was the unattended wife who had no options, no sympathy and no family to go to."

It would be hard to blame Dr. Fronske for not seeing what was brewing; after all, Marie could not or did not articulate it herself. Caspian thinks Marie was trying to reach out to him as best she could. In current psychiatric thinking, stomach problems can be linked to depression. Whether Marie was actually suffering from a physical ailment or she was trying to reach out to Dr. Fronske—or both—are more unanswered questions in the Walkup story.

While Resnick, et al., studied depressed and detached mothers, there is another disorder that has been identified more recently. In Keith Robinson's paper "No Milk Today," which recounts his findings on the Walkup murders, he wrote, "Neighbors had long whispered about Marie being a little off. She could be a little…much." To Caspian, this brought up the question of borderline personality disorder. This affliction is characterized by insecurity, impulsiveness, emotional instability and difficulty maintaining relationships. Many who suffer from this disease are terrified of being abandoned and may not do well if left alone. If Marie did have this disorder, the events of July 22 might have been predictable. Dr. Caspian speculated:

> *Someone suffering from a severe case of borderline personality disorder can become super aggressive and angry if they feel they are being abandoned…. If they feel they have no options and are being backed into a corner, suicide or murder would not be out of the question. It seems to me, in Marie's case, there was a precipitating event—something snapped. What she did was very angry, took energy and was very public. After killing her children, she drove out to the golf course—a place that speaks of money, deal-making and hobnobbing, a place her husband presumably was familiar with.*

A taphophile (or cemetery tourist) would be immediately intrigued by the Walkup children's grave marker. The plot itself is a double, with the children buried at one end. *Author's collection.*

Marie Walkup was buried at the opposite end of the plot from her children, with her head facing east, as was the custom of the day. *Author's collection.*

> *She committed suicide in a very public place; she drove out there in her nightgown to make her mark.*

Caspian finished by saying, "It's important to understand that many, many people who suffer from mental illness do fine in life if they have the protective factors. And what are those? There's access to mental health services with proper treatment, counseling and/or medications. Additionally, one needs to be with people who love and accept them as they are. Sadly, it appears Marie did not have the protective factors of love and belonging."

Whether one takes Marie Walkup's note at face value or continues to look beyond her self-confessed "failure" as the reason for her actions, we can all acknowledge that the outcome was horrific. It's difficult to contemplate now; one can only imagine how shocked and confused the town was in its aftermath. That a mother took the lives of her own flesh and blood and then her own, a woman who was well-off with a prominent family, is still hard to digest. Perhaps that is why the story is relatively unknown in Flagstaff today. After the funerals, the memories of those who died were buried deeply beneath the city's consciousness and were not welcomed back into the community at large.

I think it's fitting to end this chapter with an excerpt from the July 30, 1937 *Coconino Sun*:

> *Never before faced with so great and pathetic a tragedy, Flagstaff has been a city in mourning ever since last Friday morning when it became known. Even then it was long before it could be fully realized.*
>
> *In a few short hours a fine, conscientious, loving mother, in the absence of her husband who had left that afternoon for Phoenix on business, had strangled and stabbed the four children, and, leaving them carefully tucked in their beds at home, had driven the family car to the boundary of the Flagstaff country club golf course and there destroyed her own life with an army rifle.*
>
> *From all the facts in the case there remains no possible explanation of the quintuple tragedy except that Mrs. Walkup, morbid because of bodily ailment which apparently was not serious, and groundless fear that the children had it also, had decided before taking her own life not to leave to others the responsibility of caring for her children; or resolved to avoid death's separation by taking them with her.*[56]

After that, no mention of Marie Walkup or the Walkup children is found in the *Coconino Sun*.

Afterword

IS IT HAUNTED AND OTHER RAMBLINGS

While the previous chapter was a blend of fact and conjecture, this afterword is a medley of local anecdotes and questions that still remain. I will include my own musings, what I learned as I researched this book, a recap of that night and some of what's left unanswered.

In 2016, when researching the Walkup murders for Freaky Flagstaff Foottours, I stopped by the old house on Leroux while walking the route. The tour doesn't go within three blocks of there, but the morning was pleasant and I had the time to take a detour. I've strolled up and down the sidewalks of this wide, tree-lined street many times before. Often I'd find myself trying to imagine Marie Walkup returning home from downtown or JD enjoying the cool night air as he walked back for supper. There are pictures of Leroux from that period, and while there were fewer houses and larger yards, the street is recognizable. There's a gentle slope as you proceed northward to the home that's easy to navigate in the summer but can be slippery in the winter.

As I approached the house on this particular day, I spied a man sitting on the steps of the front porch. In previous instances when I'd deliberately walked by the place no one had been outside, either on the porch or in the yard. I screwed up my courage and approached the person, who introduced himself as Steve Rawlinson. I asked if he knew the history of the house he now occupied. To my surprise, this drew a laugh.

"What—you mean the Walkup murders? I grew up with the story. My grandparents bought this house from him back in the '30s when no one else in town would touch it."

Enthralled and with so many questions, I stood outside conversing with Steve for a good twenty minutes. He never invited me in, but he did relay a story about his daughter who had spent her childhood in the house. He told me about the day years ago when she came down to the breakfast table, took a seat and said, "Those kids were staring at me this morning."

When Steve asked her, "What kids?" she responded, "You know, those little kids that are in my bedroom closet—sometimes they come out and stare at me."

When I asked Steve if he had experienced any paranormal events in the house, he laughed and said he didn't believe in ghosts. He admitted, however, that his aunt was never comfortable in the house and refused to go upstairs. As regards his daughter's experiences, Steve said that one day he was walking through Citizens Cemetery and came upon the Walkup gravesite. As he looked at the markers, he was shocked to find that the murders-suicide occurred fifty years to the day before his daughter's birth. Perhaps, he mused, that had something to do with what she said at the table.

A few weeks later, while speaking with some people regarding the ghost tour, the Walkup house came up in conversation. A sixty-something-year-old man was surprised by the story; he had been born and raised in Flagstaff and never heard it before. I'd become used to this reaction, even from those locals with deep community roots. I gave the group a brief history, and the man's eyes grew wide.

"We used to live across the street from that house right after we were married," he said, looking at his wife for confirmation. "More than once I thought I saw a young girl chasing a ball across the side yard—she'd run around toward the front of the house and just disappear. The thing was, no children lived there that we knew of."

While this was the only story I heard of a full-blown apparition, another woman told me her daughter used to have a friend who lived in the Walkup house. The mother said she remembered the morning her little girl came back home and declared, "I'm never going back to that house. That place is haunted." The woman didn't question her any further; she said she didn't want to encourage any childish nonsense. Per usual, the mother—who had lived in Flagstaff for decades and on Leroux for a number of years—had never heard of the Walkup murders.[57]

A man who took a deep dive into the Walkup incident, Keith Robinson, was attending NAU for his graduate degree when he stumbled upon the gravesite in Citizens Cemetery. He was immediately hooked by the two markers with five names inscribed with the same date of death. We met for coffee one morning shortly before he left Flagstaff, and he brought his file folder of information, willing to share.

Keith is one of the few people I've met with whom I could unabashedly speculate on Marie's actions that day and the reasons behind them. Like forensic psychologists—which neither of us are—we have batted different theories about and tried to make sense out of the senseless. He wrote a paper, "No Milk Today," which was excerpted in the October 2019 *Daily Sun*. He then donated his work to the Special Collections unit at the NAU Library. I've relied heavily on his research several times while writing this book, as evidenced by the endnotes.

As we compared our findings over coffee that morning, I was surprised by the differences in some of our conclusions. Through that conversation and others that followed, I began to view the events of July 22, 1937, in a different light. While it's been difficult to put myself in Marie Walkup's shoes, I've tried to do so, if only to make some sense of her actions. She was from a bygone era, where women viewed themselves differently and resources for mental health were scarce. Still, she was a mother and a wife and a woman with status in the community. What could be so wrong, so broken, that murder and suicide were her answers? Following are a few of the questions that arose from my conversations with Keith and others, as well as some of the possible answers we landed on.

WHY THE COUNTRY CLUB?

As I began researching the Walkup murders for the ghost tour, the fact that Marie drove to the country club afterward to commit suicide bothered me. It made no sense. Why drive fifteen or twenty minutes north of town to kill yourself, especially after committing such a horrendous act only minutes earlier? Why not go into your own bedroom, shut the door and use either a knife or the shotgun to end your own life? If the major concern is avoiding the noise of the gun fire, it still doesn't answer the question: why the country club? That, at least, was a conscious decision.

Keith Robinson had an interesting take on Marie's choice of place. He felt that Coyote Range was perhaps the last home where Marie and JD had truly been happy. The actual road she had pulled off of and parked on was a boundary between the golf course and Dr. Colton's property. Even today it is lonesome, quiet and very dark. However, there's a beauty to the vastness of the prairie and the brilliance of the sky. Did Marie love the solitude and stillness of the land? I'd never entertained that idea before; for some reason I'd thought of her more of a city girl. Robinson's note that some neighbors found Marie "a bit much" implied a prissiness to me, but of course that need not be true.

I had come to believe Marie's choice of the club was a final middle finger toward the town that wouldn't let her in. The family car parked on the frontage road, her lifeless body with a gaping hole through the chest beside the car—did it really never cross her mind how she would be found in the morning? Flagstaff had several women's golf leagues in 1937, and like the bridge clubs, their progress was detailed in the *Sun* each week. The women were out early to get in their game; how shocking if one of the town's elite had found her body instead of the four young trespassers. What about the parties, book clubs, flower shows, bridge games, ad nauseum that filled the Personals page each week? There was no mention of Marie Walkup as part of those circles. However, many of the women golfers were and their names filled the pages. Did this influence her choice of the golf course, even subconsciously?

After speaking with Dr. Caspian and weighing Robinson's opinions, I believe the truth lies somewhere in between. Marie was a human being, and she likely harbored both a longing to be part of the community and a burning anger that she wasn't. Perhaps she had so loved the desolate prairie of Coyote Range and the years she and JD lived there that she saw the country club set as the trespassers. In her eyes were they carefree golfers playing nine holes by day then dining and dancing all the night? Maybe JD himself was nudging her to join the club—to reach out to the social elite to have an influential group of friends. Were there quiet conversations at home about the subject that Marie perceived as criticism? Or conversely, were they angry with each other, neither fulfilling the other's needs at this point in their lives? All evidence points to him as ambitious and her as reclusive.

Caspian felt strongly that shooting herself at the country club was Marie's way of "leaving a mark." I've come to feel that as well. When all has been said, it was a conscious decision on her part to end her life there.

Why That Particular Day?

I have puzzled over why Marie chose that particular Thursday to carry out her actions. The few people I've spoken with who know the Walkup history felt the event was triggered by JD leaving for Phoenix in the company of several young females. An unofficial survey among those hearing the story for the first time agreed with that assessment. The consensus is that JD was probably a bit of a "player" and Marie had put up with enough. A modern-day version of Euripides's *Medea* playing out in 1937 Flagstaff.[58]

While I leaned toward that theory at first, it has never been entirely satisfactory. If JD was indeed a philanderer, why not just divorce him and leave? While not common, divorce did occur in Flagstaff in the 1930s. Or, if the humiliation was too great to bear, why not include him in the carnage? Why did Marie kill just herself and the children? She could have killed only JD and claimed mental distress. *Medea* and exacting revenge aside, what happened that particular day or week that triggered Marie to take such drastic action?

I think it's safe to say that Marie Walkup, at least at the time of her death, was not a strong woman. It's doubtful she could have stood up to JD's looming personality if he was in fact cheating. The young bride who boarded the afternoon train, headed for adventure on a remote trading post with her new husband—that woman was gone. She had borne four children and had lived in at least five different houses in the past ten years. The man she was married to had at least one mistress—his job as a county supervisor. Marie had lived through the Great Depression and to the outside world must have seemed to be doing well. However, where was her community life? Why wasn't Marie Walkup included in any of the social events that make life bearable for any of us? The last few years of her life seem isolated and lonely, sitting inside her large family home atop the prestigious Leroux Street. While her primary role as a mother and wife was not unique for the era, something was very wrong in her life or missing entirely.

JD Walkup is not here to defend himself, so I can only speculate on whether he was cheating on his wife. While many people feel he was, I've gone back and forth on this issue and landed in the camp that thinks he was a faithful, if preoccupied, husband. I came to that conclusion for a number of reasons, not the least being how difficult it is to keep a secret in Flagstaff today with a population of eighty thousand. News travels fast up here. If there was a whisper of scandal in 1937, it would have spread like a wildfire among the tiny town of five thousand. While I couldn't find the source again this year, I have read that JD was *asked* if he'd chauffeur the lady ballplayers to Phoenix that Thursday. Given the distance and torturous route back then, the request only makes sense. Perhaps the rumors that Walkup was a philanderer grew legs when he and Doris Gee, one of the young women in the tournament, married a decade later. By then, however, JD was living in the Phoenix area. There's also no evidence that Gee was one of the young women JD gave a ride to that fateful day.

JD belonged to the Masons and the Knights of Pythias. Both organizations stressed good moral character and sobriety as a way of life. While this guarantees nothing, it does speak to how Walkup wanted to be aligned. I've come to believe that he saw himself as a principled man and tried to live his life as such.

I do have one more thought on what might have precipitated the events of July 22, 1937. Could Marie Walkup have thought she was pregnant? It's unclear if the "chronic" stomach ailment had been ongoing for a month or a year. If she'd only been calling Dr. Fronske for several weeks, it's possible Marie thought it was morning sickness. It's obvious in retrospect she was struggling with depression; the prospect of another child might have driven her to a breaking point. No autopsy was performed, so that is a question that will be left unanswered. It's not hard to imagine that another pregnancy, a husband chauffeuring young women to Phoenix and the prospect of a lonely existence in the decades to come formed a perfect storm in the young mother's mind.

What Happened That Evening?

Another question I have grappled with and one that will inevitably be left unanswered is: how did she manage to stab and strangle four children without one or more escaping? It was midsummer in Flagstaff—some form of daylight would have been evident until 8:00 p.m. The older children were seen outside Thursday afternoon, and baby Elizabeth was last seen alive in the late afternoon. All four death certificates state death occurred "about 8 to 9 p.m." The children's time of death was based partly on Marie's phone call to Dr. Fronske's home at 10:00 p.m. While it makes sense that the children had been killed before the call, it doesn't answer why a ten-year-old, eight-year-old and four-year-old were so profoundly asleep at 9:00 p.m. in the summer.

I have questioned whether Marie could have used a drug to sedate the children earlier in the evening. Paregoric, an opium-based medication, was once commonly prescribed for stomach ailments. A bottle of it might have been available due to Marie's intestinal complaints. Perhaps she gave each child a healthy dose at supper, assuring that they'd sleep deeply that night.

The two bedrooms were at opposite ends of the one-and-a-half-story bungalow. Daniel and baby Elizabeth were downstairs and at the back of the house; Rose and John were upstairs in the bedroom facing south. The stone fireplace that abutted Daniel's room and the staircase would have insulated against muffled cries echoing through the wooden structure. Surely Marie took the additional precaution of closing bedroom doors that night.

There's good evidence that at least one child, Rose Marie, woke up during the attack when the icepick deflected off of her rib rather than piercing her heart. The hurried account of the murders in Friday's *Sun* contained some confusion regarding timing of events, as well as vague explanations. To wit, this sentence appeared in connection with the coroner's jury: "There were bruise marks on the throats of three, and on the throat of one a slight laceration, as though from a fingernail."

The *Arizona Republic* put it more bluntly: "With the exception of Rose Marie, whose body indicated she had awakened and resisted her mother, the children all died without struggling."

It's never made clear whose throat bore just a "slight laceration." Surely that didn't refer to Rose. From the evidence, she awoke after the first, misplaced stab, and the mother was forced to grapple with her daughter as she strangled her to death. I'd think there would be scratches, welts and extensive bruising noted on the little girl's neck after such a struggle. With her siblings, the strangling came *after* the mortal wounds to the chest.

Was little Rose the last to die? In every retelling of the story, Elizabeth and John were the first to be killed. Marie then walked up the stairs to the second bedroom and finished what she had begun that night. There is no evidence that the murders were actually carried out in that order.

One bizarre aspect of that evening that hasn't been described in detail is the crime scene inside the house. As written earlier, the children were all found in their respective beds. They appeared clean and the bedding was fresh and each was covered with a sheet pulled up to the chin. There were no outward signs of violence, at least on initial inspection. It wasn't until later, when the coroner's jury returned to the home on Leroux to investigate further, that the full horror of the rampage was revealed. Stashed inside the fireplace in the living room was a brown woolen blanket that was folded into a bundle. Opening it, the men found all the items Marie had attempted to hide: the blood-soaked bedding and towels, the children's night clothes and the murder weapon itself, a bloody icepick. With this discovery the jury pieced together the events of the night as best they could.

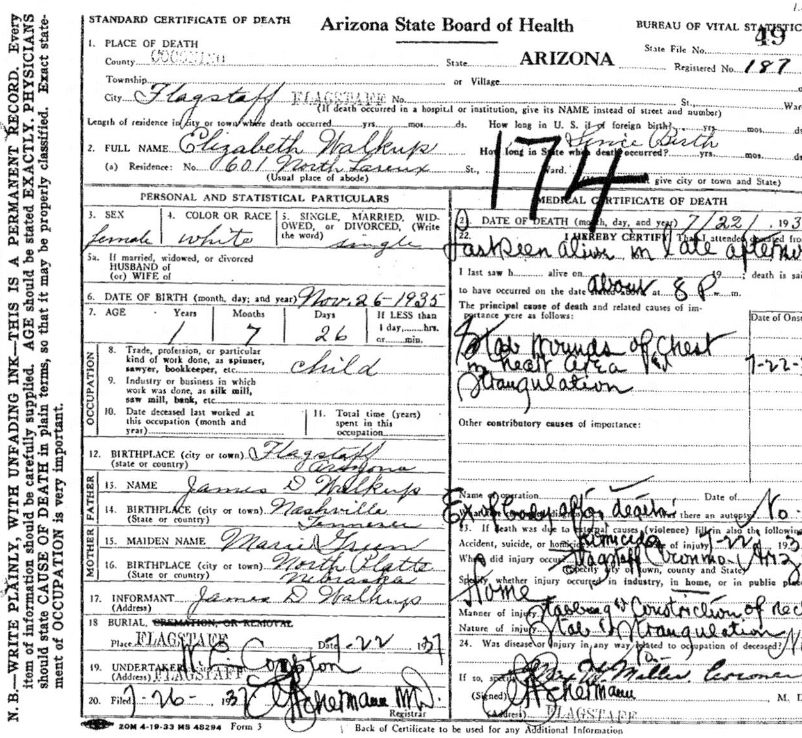

N. B.—WRITE PLAINLY, WITH UNFADING INK—THIS IS A PERMANENT RECORD. Every item of information should be carefully supplied. AGE should be stated EXACTLY. PHYSICIANS should state CAUSE OF DEATH in plain terms, so that it may be properly classified. Exact statement of OCCUPATION is very important.

MARGIN RESERVED FOR BINDING

STANDARD CERTIFICATE OF DEATH

Arizona State Board of Health

BUREAU OF VITAL STATISTICS

49

State File No.

Registered No. 187

1. PLACE OF DEATH
County COCONINO State ARIZONA
Township or Village
City Flagstaff FLAGSTAFF No. St., Ward
(If death occurred in a hospital or institution, give its NAME instead of street and number)
Length of residence in city or town where death occurred ... yrs. ... mos. ... ds. How long in U. S. if of foreign birth? ... yrs. ... mos. ... ds.

2. FULL NAME Elizabeth Walkup — How long in State when death occurred? Since Birth ... yrs. ... mos. ... ds.
(a) Residence: No. 601 North Leroux St., Ward
(Usual place of abode) (If nonresident give city or town and State)

174

PERSONAL AND STATISTICAL PARTICULARS

3. SEX female
4. COLOR OR RACE white
5. SINGLE, MARRIED, WIDOWED, or DIVORCED, (Write the word) single
5a. If married, widowed, or divorced HUSBAND of (or) WIFE of
6. DATE OF BIRTH (month, day; and year) Nov. 26 1935
7. AGE Years 1 Months 7 Days 26 If LESS than 1 day, ... hrs. or ... min.

OCCUPATION
8. Trade, profession, or particular kind of work done, as spinner, sawyer, bookkeeper, etc. child
9. Industry or business in which work was done, as silk mill, saw mill, bank, etc.
10. Date deceased last worked at this occupation (month and year)
11. Total time (years) spent in this occupation

12. BIRTHPLACE (city or town) Flagstaff (state or country) Arizona

FATHER
13. NAME James D Walkup
14. BIRTHPLACE (city or town) Nashville (State or country) Tennessee

MOTHER
15. MAIDEN NAME Marie Green
16. BIRTHPLACE (city or town) North Platte (State or country) Nebraska

17. INFORMANT James D Walkup (Address)
18. BURIAL, ~~CREMATION, OR REMOVAL~~ Place FLAGSTAFF Date 7-22 1937
19. UNDERTAKER W. C. Compton (Address) FLAGSTAFF
20. Filed 7-26- 1937 Ackermann M.D. Registrar

MEDICAL CERTIFICATE OF DEATH

21. DATE OF DEATH (month, day, and year) 7/22/1937
22. I HEREBY CERTIFY, That I attended deceased from
Last seen alive in late afternoon
I last saw h... alive on ... 19...; death is said to have occurred on the date stated above at about 8 P. m.
The principal cause of death and related causes of importance were as follows: Date of Onset
Stab wounds of chest in heart area — Strangulation — 7-22-37

Other contributory causes of importance:

Name of operation ... Date of ...
What test confirmed diagnosis? Ex. of body after death. Was there an autopsy? No.

23. If death was due to external causes (violence) fill in also the following:
Accident, suicide, or homicide? Homicide Date of injury 7-22 1937
Where did injury occur? Flagstaff Coconino Ariz.
(Specify city or town, county and State)
Specify whether injury occurred in industry, in home, or in public place. Home
Manner of injury Stabbing & Constriction of neck
Nature of injury Stab & Strangulation
24. Was disease or injury in any way related to occupation of deceased? No.
If so, specify
Miller Coroner
(Signed) Ackermann, M. D.
(Address) FLAGSTAFF

20M 4-19-33 MS 48294 Form 3 — Back of Certificate to be used for any Additional Information

Note that on Elizabeth's death certificate she was last seen alive in the late afternoon. There was no autopsy, just an examination of the body. *Courtesy K. Renner.*

Their belief was that Marie Walkup, in the throes of anxiety over a nonexistent ailment, put her children to bed early Thursday evening. Around 9:00 p.m. she entered the downstairs bedroom, stabbing Elizabeth twice in the chest before strangling her. She then turned her attention toward John, who was asleep in his bed in the same room. She proceeded to stab her son twice in the chest area and then strangle him, possibly with a man's handkerchief knotted on both ends. This homemade garrote or tourniquet was mentioned only once in the *Sun*, and its purpose in the killings is speculative.[59]

Well past the point of no return Marie exited the downstairs bedroom and turned left to enter the living room. Crossing the great room, she veered right toward the kitchen area and then mounted the narrow staircase. On the second floor landing she once again turned left and opened the door of the south bedroom. She entered John and Rose Marie's room—icepick and possibly tourniquet in hand—and approached John's bed. Repeating

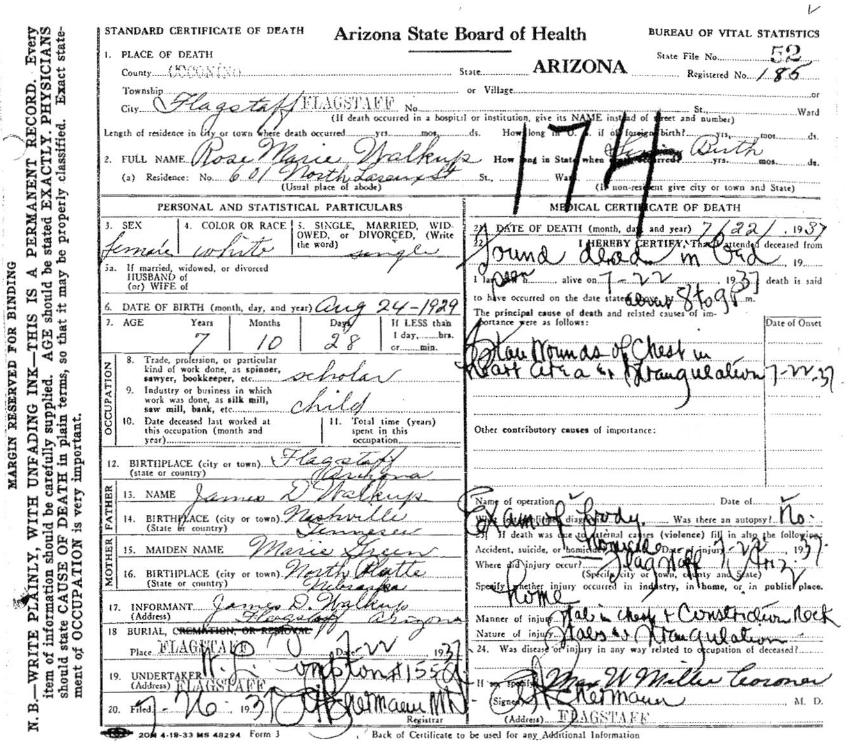

N. B.—WRITE PLAINLY, WITH UNFADING INK—THIS IS A PERMANENT RECORD. Every item of information should be carefully supplied. AGE should be stated EXACTLY. PHYSICIANS should state CAUSE OF DEATH in plain terms, so that it may be properly classified. Exact statement of OCCUPATION is very important.

MARGIN RESERVED FOR BINDING

STANDARD CERTIFICATE OF DEATH — Arizona State Board of Health — BUREAU OF VITAL STATISTICS

1. PLACE OF DEATH — County: Coconino — State: ARIZONA — State File No. 52 — Registered No. 186

City: Flagstaff FLAGSTAFF

2. FULL NAME: Rose Marie Walkup

(a) Residence: No. 601 North Leroux St

PERSONAL AND STATISTICAL PARTICULARS

3. SEX: female — 4. COLOR OR RACE: white — 5. SINGLE, MARRIED, WIDOWED, or DIVORCED: single

6. DATE OF BIRTH: Aug 24-1929

7. AGE: Years 7, Months 10, Days 28

8. Trade, profession, or particular kind of work done: scholar

9. Industry or business in which work was done: child

12. BIRTHPLACE: Flagstaff, Arizona

FATHER — 13. NAME: James D. Walkup — 14. BIRTHPLACE: Nashville, Tennessee

MOTHER — 15. MAIDEN NAME: Marie Green — 16. BIRTHPLACE: North Platte, Nebraska

17. INFORMANT: James D. Walkup, Flagstaff, Arizona

18. BURIAL — Place: FLAGSTAFF — Date: 7-22 1937

19. UNDERTAKER: FLAGSTAFF

20. Filed 7-26-1937 — Registrar

MEDICAL CERTIFICATE OF DEATH

21. DATE OF DEATH: 7/22/1937

22. I HEREBY CERTIFY, That I attended deceased from: Found dead in bed

alive on 7-22 1937; death is said to have occurred on the date stated above at about 8 to 9 p.m.

The principal cause of death and related causes of importance were as follows: Stab wounds of chest in heart area & strangulation 7-22-37

Was there an autopsy? No

Accident, suicide, or homicide? Homicide — Date of injury 7-22 1937

Where did injury occur? Flagstaff, Ariz.

Specify whether injury occurred in industry, in home, or in public place: Home

Manner of injury: Stab in chest & constriction neck

Nature of injury: Stabs & strangulation

(Signed) Max W. Miller Coroner — (Address) FLAGSTAFF

Form 3 — Back of Certificate to be used for any Additional Information

The children's death certificates all stated they were found in their beds and death was attributed to stab wounds to the chest and strangulation. On Rose's, the coroner wrote "about 8 to 9 p.m." as the time of death. *Courtesy Karen Renner.*

her actions from before, Marie stabbed the young boy twice in the chest and then strangled him.

Whether Rose was awakened by a noise or was blessedly unaware until the icepick hit her rib, it was determined she did wake up after the first blow and struggled with her mother. I suspect the latter is the case. It's hard to imagine an eight-year-old lying passively in bed awaiting an attack, even from her own mother. One would think some sort of survival instinct would kick in. Regardless, when the pick deflected off her rib, Rose raised her hands to fend off another attack. Marie either choked her daughter with her bare hands or used the knotted handkerchief to complete the killing. The fingernail imprint reported by the *Sun* is taken by many to indicate Rose resisted and fought with Marie, although that is only speculation. In the end, she was no match against her mother's strength and determination. It's particularly difficult to try to imagine Rose's final moments—eyes locked with those of Marie, fighting to loosen the grip on her neck, unable to breathe and, finally, succumbing to the attack.

After the killings were done, Marie set about the task of cleaning her home and bathing the children one last time. Whether she carried their bodies to the bathtub or gave them a bed bath is unknown; however, each child's body was washed and then dressed in clean pajamas. The blood-soaked linen was stripped and thrown into the brown bundle, then each bed remade with fresh sheets. The children were laid out in his or her own bed, sheets pulled up to the chin, with a small teddy bear propped up under baby Elizabeth's chin.

It was speculated that the 10:30 p.m. call to Dr. Fronske's home came after the killings and cleanup. Marie would have then written the four letters found on site, placing the two addressed to her husband and mother in the house and the remaining two outside on the porch. In Robinson's paper, he writes:

> *Marie sat down at the dining room table with a pen and pink stationary. She had to think now. To focus. In clear, neat, carefully considered penmanship, she began to write the first of four maddeningly ambiguous letters. The first was for the milkman, a missive she would slip into an empty milk bottle and leave on the front porch for him to discover in the morning. The second, which she nailed to the front door, was addressed to Dr. Fronske. The third was jointly addressed to Marie's mother and her sister…it contained instructions about what should be done with various personal items of Marie's. This note was left on the dining room table. The fourth and final note, which Marie stuck in a desk drawer near the front door, was addressed to her husband.*

Robinson goes on to describe the orderliness inside the home and what likely followed the notes:

> *The dinner dishes had been cleared, washed and stored. Everything was in its place; the house was orderly. Dressed only in her nightgown and slippers, Marie walked toward the back of the house.…When she reached the closet in her and James' downstairs bedroom, she reached up and grabbed his rusty old army rifle, a .30-06 Springfield, tucked it under her arm, went out the front door.*

The coroner's report stated Marie had committed suicide "shortly before midnight." Given the time it would have taken to write four letters, place

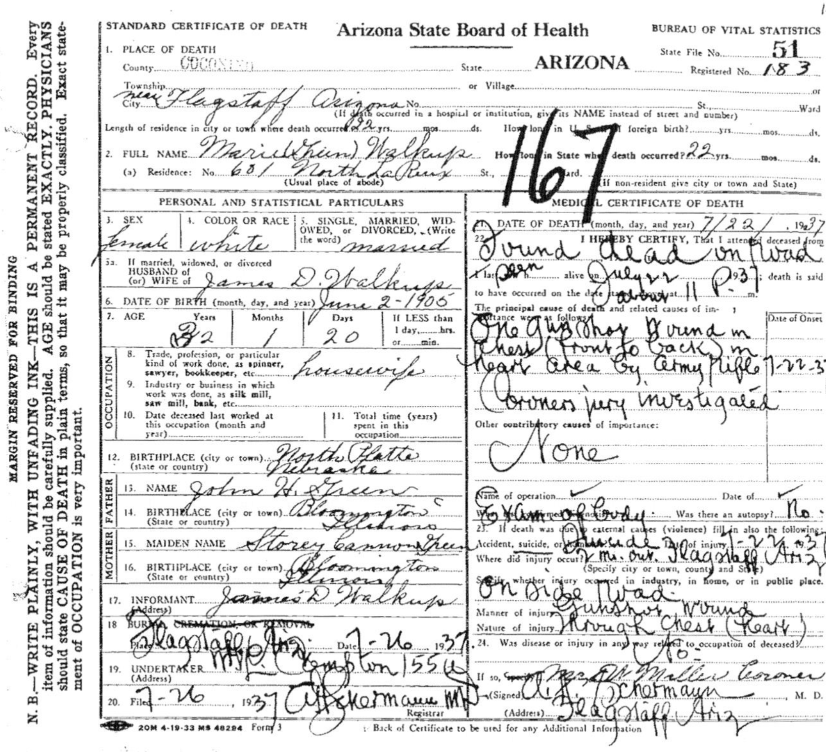

N. B.—WRITE PLAINLY, WITH UNFADING INK—THIS IS A PERMANENT RECORD. Every item of information should be carefully supplied. AGE should be stated EXACTLY. PHYSICIANS should state CAUSE OF DEATH in plain terms, so that it may be properly classified. Exact statement of OCCUPATION is very important.

MARGIN RESERVED FOR BINDING

STANDARD CERTIFICATE OF DEATH — Arizona State Board of Health — BUREAU OF VITAL STATISTICS — ARIZONA

State File No. 51 — Registered No. 183

1. PLACE OF DEATH — County Coconino — State ARIZONA — Township or Village — City near Flagstaff Arizona — No. — St. — Ward (If death occurred in a hospital or institution, give its NAME instead of street and number)

Length of residence in city or town where death occurred 32 yrs. — How long in U. S., if of foreign birth? — How long in State where death occurred? 22 yrs.

2. FULL NAME Marie (Green) Walkup — (a) Residence: No. 601 North LaRoux St. (Usual place of abode) (If non-resident give city or town and State)

167

PERSONAL AND STATISTICAL PARTICULARS

3. SEX female — 4. COLOR OR RACE white — 5. SINGLE, MARRIED, WIDOWED, or DIVORCED (Write the word) married

5a. If married, widowed, or divorced HUSBAND of (or) WIFE of James D. Walkup

6. DATE OF BIRTH (month, day, and year) June 2-1905

7. AGE Years 32 Months 1 Days 20 — If LESS than 1 day, ...hrs. or ...min.

8. Trade, profession, or particular kind of work done, as spinner, sawyer, bookkeeper, etc. housewife

9. Industry or business in which work was done, as silk mill, saw mill, bank, etc.

10. Date deceased last worked at this occupation (month and year) — 11. Total time (years) spent in this occupation

12. BIRTHPLACE (city or town) (state or country) North Platte Nebraska

FATHER — 13. NAME John H. Green — 14. BIRTHPLACE (city or town) (State or country) Bloomington Illinois

MOTHER — 15. MAIDEN NAME Storey Cannon Green — 16. BIRTHPLACE (city or town) (State or country) Bloomington Illinois

17. INFORMANT James D. Walkup (Address)

18. BURIAL, ~~CREMATION, OR REMOVAL~~ Place Flagstaff Ariz. Date 7-26 1937

19. UNDERTAKER (Address) M. P. Compton 1551

20. Filed 7-26, 1937 — A. F. Ackermann MD Registrar

MEDICAL CERTIFICATE OF DEATH

21. DATE OF DEATH (month, day, and year) 7/22/, 1937

22. I HEREBY CERTIFY, That I attended deceased from Found dead on road — I last saw h... alive on July 22 1937 — death is said to have occurred on the date stated above, at about 11 P. m.

The principal cause of death and related causes of importance were as follows: One gun shot wound in chest (front to back) in heart area by army rifle — Date of Onset 7-22-37.

Coroners jury investigated

Other contributory causes of importance: None

Name of operation — Date of — What test confirmed diagnosis? Exam of body — Was there an autopsy? No.

23. If death was due to external causes (violence) fill in also the following: Accident, suicide, or homicide Suicide — Date of injury 7-22-37. Where did injury occur? 2 mi. out. Flagstaff Ariz. (Specify city or town, county and State)

Specify whether injury occurred in industry, in home, or in public place. On side road

Manner of injury Gunshot wound — Nature of injury through chest (heart)

24. Was disease or injury in any way related to occupation of deceased? No.

If so, specify — Mr. J. W. Miller Coroner — (Signed) A. F. Ackermann, M. D. — (Address) Flagstaff Ariz

20M 4-19-33 MS 48294 Form 3 — Back of Certificate to be used for any Additional Information

Marie's death certificate adds little to our understanding of the tragedy. She was last seen on July 22, and she shot herself at approximately 11:00 p.m. that night. There was no autopsy. *Courtesy Karen Renner.*

them, check the house one more time then retrieve the rifle and drive three miles to the country club, the sequence of events appears to be right. If the tragedy occurred today forensic science could tell us the order of the stabbings, an accurate time of death and whether the children were drugged. An autopsy would have revealed if Marie Walkup was pregnant at the time. Modern CSI could recreate the murders and possibly expound on Rose Marie's final moments—the extent she fought back and her actual cause of death. However, the Walkup family murders-suicide occurred in 1937, and a stunned town was not inclined to investigate any further than necessary.

While writing this book, I sometimes felt I had embarked on a journey akin to an emotional roller coaster. There were days I was immersed in research that left me empty and frustrated after five hours of scrolling. Where was Marie Green Walkup before July 22, 1937? Because of the COVID-19 pandemic and the various restrictions, I relied heavily on online resources. While I might have found more material if I could have scoured the libraries myself, I'm uncertain as to how much more. I've been interested in the Walkup family for well over a decade and had already done some sleuthing. Information on Marie and the children is hard to come by.

I'd like to close the book on the Walkup family tragedy with a few observations and final thoughts. The *Coconino Sun* was a great resource and, for all my criticisms, a real treasure as a community newspaper. It faithfully covered the town it served with honesty, humor and a generous dollop of puritanical judgement. The front page was a mixture of local, state and national news that was well-written and relevant to the time. The opinion page was filled with pithy observations that revealed the proud self-reliance of the writers and their audience. The society section, which occasionally irritated me because of who and what was missing, told the story of a generous, fun-loving community that supported one another in the decades surrounding the Depression. It's so easy to fall into the trap of characterizing an era with one-dimensional epitaphs. While I never met the people on the *Sun*'s pages, I gained a sense of their quirks and humanity through the odd bits of information that were written.

When talking with Dr. Caspian, I confided in her that I was sometimes irritated with the town that seemingly snubbed this woman and left her desperate. While my frustration was real, championing Marie so many decades later is based only on assumptions. JD Walkup was a large figure who rode into town in 1922 and immersed himself in the life he found in Flagstaff. Marie Green arrived here in 1916 at age eleven and not a peep was heard from or about her until she married JD in June 1925. JD's presence grew as he joined clubs, ran for office and generally inserted himself into the town's civic life. As for Marie, one can't really even say her life waned because there's no public baseline on her as a person. In the end, it's just as reasonable to assume she shunned the town as the reverse.

If Marie was an enigma, the children might as well have been ghosts. The Boy Scouts and Girl Scouts had formed troops in Flagstaff about a decade prior but neither John nor Rose was listed on the rosters. The *Sun* continued to cover the elementary schools in the 1930s, printing kudos for perfect attendance, high math scores, et cetera. I never found a mention of the Walkup children regarding this or any other activity. Perhaps they truly were undisciplined, as Marie alluded to in her note to JD. She might not have had the energy to correct them, especially in the final years. It was sad that none of the Walkup children were named as attending the birthday parties and other celebrations for children their age. The fact that these parties were covered on the society page—with as much detail as given the adult fetes—must have been hurtful to those who were excluded as well as their parents.

Ultimately, the mystery of the Walkup family tragedy lies in the darkness and unknowingness that surround them. In this book, I tried to find answers to the questions that plagued me about the Walkups and the town that buried them. While I have come away with an overall appreciation of life in Flagstaff in the early twentieth century and a feel for Marie and her family, many questions remain. What we know for sure is that on a clear summer night in July 1937, Marie Walkup took the lives of her four children and then drove north to the country club at the outskirts of town. There, under a canopy of brilliant stars and a full moon, she took her own life as well, leaving a small mountain town to wonder why in the darkness.

NOTES

Introduction

1. Cline, *Mountain Town*. This book provided much of the background information on Flagstaff throughout the early twentieth century. Cline was the editor of the *Daily Sun*, the newspaper that succeeded the weekly *Coconino Sun*. He wrote two books on Flagstaff (the other being *They Came to the Mountain*) that are excellent reading for anyone interested in how the city was shaped and formed. Many of the details on 1930s Flagstaff came from Chapter 13.
2. As with much of this book, I was informed on the weekly events and goings-on in the town by reading through decades of the *Coconino Sun*. While other sources were also used, it was on the *Sun*'s personal pages or in the social columns that I found detailed reporting on what parties, charities, teas or pastimes were in vogue. Since some of the background writing is a compilation of a year's worth of newspaper reporting, I can't credit just one issue.
3. While I was certain Platt Cline was the one who dubbed Leroux "Knob Hill," I could not relocate the source. However, Richard and Sherry Magnum also made the reference when referring to the former Pollock home in their book, *Flagstaff, Past & Present*, on page 107.

Chapter 1

4. There are several good books on Flagstaff's early history besides the two by Cline. *Flagstaff Past & Present* by Richard and Sherry Magnum not only recaps the early days of Beale and the railroad but it's also full of great photographs. *Flagstaff*

Memories, the Early Years was put together in 2017 by the *Daily Sun* and also creates a pictorial narrative of the town. As said before, the historical information of the town's beginnings overlaps in all these fine books, so it's impossible to credit one as a source. I should also note that this incredible land was held sacred by various Native American tribes long before the white man came and settled with his livestock. When I write "early history" of the town I am truly referring to late 1800s to early 1900s Flagstaff. It is beyond my scope and ability to detail the various tribes who lived here for centuries before Beale came through.

5. Riordan Mansion State Historic Park was closed in 2020 due to COVID-19 but is hopefully open by the time this book is published. Self-guided tours through the outside gardens are free and inside tours of the house are relatively inexpensive as well as fascinating. The Riordans were visionaries in many ways, and they also believed in investing in their community. The house and grounds contain implements used in the logging business as well as toys, excerpts from writings and lots of pictures from the early twentieth century.
6. James E. Babbitt co-authored an Images of America book on Flagstaff, which has great pictures of the Babbitt family's mercantile store, as well as many of the town itself.

Chapter 2

7. Much of the information I found on Thelma Marie Green came from the rare newspaper account prior to July 22, 1937, and was always in connection to her marriage to JD. Relying on issues of the *Coconino Sun* from 1916 to 1927, I deduced some background material on the Green family by what wasn't printed.
8. *Coconino Sun*, 1916–24.
9. *Coconino Sun* issues. Interestingly, up to and through the early 1920s, students at Emerson School were reported by name as getting 100 percent in spelling or math, perfect attendance, not being tardy, et cetera. These little reports usually appeared twice a month in the paper, with holiday programs garnering a special column. Marie's sister's name appeared at least once but never Marie's.
10. *Coconino Sun*, November 2, 1934.
11. Cline, *Mountain Town*, 323. This is the only mention of JD Walkup in Cline's book and it's in conjunction with finding a source of municipal water. Cline mentions Walkup's credibility as a war hero, which was significant for the time.

Chapter 3

12. As of this writing in 2020, one can find the weekly issues of the *Coconino Sun* from 1898 to 1927 online at either the Library of Congress Chronicling America site

or through Newspapers.com. All issues of the *Sun* are available at the Flagstaff Public Library on microfilm, where I spent hours researching before the COVID pandemic forced it to close its doors.

13. One source of information on both Cline and the *Daily Sun* is a short tribute written to both in Kevin Schindler and Michael Kitt's book, *Historic Tales of Flagstaff*. While Cline was actually born in Colorado, the former editor and publisher earned the name "Mr. Flagstaff" for the many ways he benefitted his adopted hometown.

Chapter 4

14. *Coconino Sun*, June 19, 1925, 16.
15. Ibid., August 1, 1924, 1. Flagstaff had more than one team in 1924. The game reported on in the cited issue occurred on Sunday, July 27, and was between the Babbitt Cannibals and the Flagstaff Independents. According to the article, "The Flagstaff Independents handed the Babbitt baseball team the short end of the total at city park on Sunday. Each inning had its share of disputes which each time threatened to stop the game. Both teams are to have meetings Monday night and decide who will do the arguing in the next game." Walkup played second base most of that year.
16. Ibid., June 27, 1924, 1. While several descriptions of the Navajo squaw dance can be found, the one written up in this issue of the *Sun* is excellent.
17. Ibid., October 12, 1923, 1. As said before, Zane Grey was a frequent visitor to the town and was often interviewed by the newspaper. This particular article quoted Grey as pushing for more hotels, as the citizenry didn't realize how quickly tourism would explode in the town. If one reads just the *Sun*'s front pages that year it's evident that tourist dollars, conventioneers and a larger, more dependable source of water was on everyone's mind.
18. Cline, *Mountain Town*, 362.
19. *Coconino Sun*, December 19, 1924, 11. The brief item read, in part, "Mrs. H.C. Metz presided over a very attractively appointed Christmas dinner party Monday night for four of the city teachers and guests, who took in the play at the Normal and finished up the evening at Five Hundred. The guests were Misses Lucile Bigham, Lucile Snyder, Mary Fullington and Margaret Schumaker, and James Walkup, Corliss Perry, Hill H. Lewis and Clyde Merchon."
20. Ibid., January 23, 1925, 1.
21. Ibid.
22. Ibid., February 27, 1925, 11.
23. Ibid., July 23, 1937. The brief mention of Marie living with the Pollocks was found in the write-up of her death. I found no information on when or in what capacity she stayed with the family.

Chapter 5

24. Ibid., June 19, 1925, 16. On page 15 of the same issue, this blurb appeared under the Local Brevities: "Jim Walkup came in from the Cibicue trading post, of which he is manager and minister extraordinary to the Apaches, on general post business and to make some local arrangements for a big Fourth celebration the Apaches will put on at Cibicue."
25. Information on Cibicue was gathered from Wikipedia, old trail maps and a road trip.
26. *Coconino Sun,* February 5, 1926, 2; February 26, 1926, 2. The item ran on the Local Brevities page: "Mrs. Jim Walkup returned last week to Cibicue to join her husband, factor [*sic*] there for Babbitts. She spent a couple of weeks here as the guest of Miss Alice Brown."
27. Ibid., September 24, 1926, 2.
28. *Coconino Sun,* May 13, 1927, 1. As mentioned several times in this book, Flagstaff is considered a small town today, even as our population nears 80,000. In 1927, there were fewer than 3,500 people, and the geographic location made travel difficult—for people! News in the town traveled quickly, and one has to imagine Frank Brooks was aware of Walkup's new venture. When reading the two papers (May 13 and May 20) in sequence I had to smile and wonder if this was Brooks's preemptive strike against his former employee.

Chapter 6

29. Cline, *Mountain Town,* 293. Chapter 13 of Cline's book is titled "Hard Times Along the River De Flagg" and is an in-depth recounting of how the Great Depression affected the town, it's people and various institutions.
30. *Coconino Sun,* November 2, 1934.
31. Robinson, "No Milk Today." In his paper, Robinson details the time he spent researching the Walkups' backgrounds, including JD's time at Colton's ranch. The phone number is the only mention of Walkup that he found. I was not able to duplicate his research at the Colton's library so relied on his account.
32. *Coconino Sun,* November 2, 1934. As far as documenting Marie's lack of civic involvement, I did this by what I *did not* find in the rosters and participants of various clubs.
33. Ibid.

Chapter 7

34. Cline, *Mountain Town,* 305–26. In the same chapter 13 cited previously, "Hard Times Along the River De Flagg," Cline details the mechanics of how Flagstaff

dug its way out of the Depression, not only with federal assistance but also by coming together as a community.

35. *Coconino Sun*, January 4, 1935, 1

36. Ibid., 1935.

37. Ibid. Besides reading through issues of the *Sun*, some background information comes from Cline's *Mountain Town*, as well as information gleaned from tours of Riordan Mansion and the historic tours once given by the Magnums.

38. *Coconino Sun*, June–July 1937, 1. There was a big buildup to the Powwow that year and plenty of articles reporting on various details, all front-page. Also, I found two different spellings of the event through the years and depending on the publication. I went with "Powwow," but some spelled it "Pow Wow."

Chapter 8

39. All of the information found in this chapter—except where specifically noted—is taken from the pages of the *Coconino Sun* from July 1937 and Keith Robinson's paper, "No Milk Today." As Robinson also used the *Sun*'s account of what occurred, the source and information are entwined.

40. "Good Roads Everywhere."

41. Rogers, "Interview with Billie and Ernest."

42. Once again, I have borrowed heavily from Robinson's paper, especially in the telling of the hikers.

43. *Arizona Republic*, July 23, 1937, 1.

44. I found references to the murders-suicide in the *Los Angeles Times*, *Chicago Tribune*, *Washington Times*, *Salt Lake Tribune* and newspapers in Europe, Australia and Canada.

45. *Coconino Sun*, July 30, 1937, 1. The murders-suicide were covered in the July 23 edition of the *Sun*; the aftermath, including the funerals, were covered the following week.

Chapter 9

46. *Coconino Sun*, May–September 1938.

47. Ibid., January–November 1939. From mid-1938 through 1940 is where COVID-19 had the greatest impact on my research. Although the local librarians were extremely helpful when given specific dates to check the *Sun* or other documents for information, they didn't have the time to shift through the microfilm as I did pre-pandemic. I'm certain that—when the library opens again—I'll find the answers to so many questions that popped up as I put together JD's timeline after the tragedy. Even hard copies of the *Coconino Sun* were impossible to track

down, and the later issues on microfilm (1928–46) are only available at Flagstaff Public Library.
48. Robinson, "No Milk Today."

Chapter 10

49. West, "An Overview of Filicide," 48–47.
50. Friedman and Resnick, "Child Murder by Mothers," 137–41. I found several papers on maternal filicide and almost all point to Dr. Resnick as the first professional to give the phenomenon serious study. My observation was confirmed by Dr. Elizabeth Caspian, a psychiatrist interviewed for this book.
51. Friedman, Holden, et al. "Maternal Filicide and Its Intersection with Suicide."
52. *Coconino Sun*, July 23, 1937, 1.
53. Ibid.
54. *Arizona Republic*, July 23, 1937, 1.
55. I spoke with Dr. Elizabeth Caspian on November 23, 2020. She was generous with her time and was gracious enough to indulge my speculation while lending a professional restraint to the conversation. Dr. Caspian had read the three papers I cited (as well as several others to refresh her knowledge) and added so much to the overall understanding of a tragic event.
56. *Coconino Sun*, July 30, 1937, 1.

Afterword

57. Several years ago, I ran into the woman and her daughter completely by chance. When I asked the young woman, now an adult, about the incident that happened decades earlier, she said she could not remember it. However, she did agree "that house was really creepy."
58. All of the tour guides for the ghost tours have noticed that—besides being a disturbing story—the tale invariably generates speculation and discussion over the question of *why*.
59. The summary of events from the night of July 22, 1937, come from *Coconino Sun*, July 23, 1937, 1, and Robinson, "No Milk Today."

BIBLIOGRAPHY

Newspapers

Arizona Republic
Coconino Sun

Interviews

Caspian, Elizabeth, MD. Phone interview with author, November 23, 2020.

Books and Articles/Papers

Babbitt, James E., and John G. DeGraff III. *Flagstaff*. Charleston, SC: Arcadia Publishing, 2009.

Cline, Platt. *Mountain Town, Flagstaff's First Century*. Flagstaff, AZ: Northland Publishing, 1994.

Friedman, Susan, MD; Carol Holden, Ph.D; Debra Hrouda, MSSA; and Phillip J. Resnick, MD. "Maternal Filicide and Its Intersection with Suicide." *Brief Treatment and Crisis Intervention* 8 (April 9, 2008): 283–29. doi:10.1093/brief-treatment/mhn011.

Friedman, Susan, and Phillip Resnick. "Child Murders by Mothers: Patterns and Prevention." *World Psychiatry* 6 (2007): 137–41. www.ncbi.nim.nih.gov.

Mangum, Richard, and Sherry Mangum. *Flagstaff Past & Present*. Flagstaff, AZ: Northland Publishing, 2003.

Robinson, Keith. "No Milk Today." February 16, 2019.

Schindler, Kevin, and Michael Kitt. *Historic Tales of Flagstaff*. Charleston, SC: The History Press, 2019.

West, Sara G., MD. "An Overview of Filicide." *Psychiatry* 4, no. 2 (February 2007): 48–57. www.ncbi.nim.nih.gov.

Websites

Arizona Department of Transportation. "Good Roads Everywhere: A History of Road Building in Arizona." May 2003. www.azdot.gov.

Flagstaff Public Library. "Pow Wow Exhibit." Online Resources. *Souvenir Program Southwest All Indian Pow Wow,* July 2, 3, 4, 1939. www.flagstaffpubliclibrary.org.

Kawarsky, Irvin. "The Evolution and History of Softball in the United States." Steve Dimitry's Softball History Website. 1998. www.angelfire.com.

Library of Congress. "Chronicling America—Historic American Newspapers." *Coconino Sun*. https://chroniclingamerica.loc.gov.

Miklich, E., comp. 19C Baseball. 2016. www.19Cbaseball.com.

Rogers, Susan. "Interview with Billie and Ernest Yost." Cline Library. Flagstaff Public Library Oral History Project. NAU Special Collections. November 21, 1975. www.archive.library.nau.edu.